THE LIFE AND FAITH OF
THE BAPTISTS

"If you will go with us, you must go against wind and tide; the which, I perceive, is against your opinion. You must also own Religion in his rags, as well as when in his silver slippers; and stand by him, too, when bound in irons, as well as when he walketh the streets with applause."

Christian to By-ends, in "The Pilgrim's Progress"

THE LIFE AND FAITH
OF THE BAPTISTS

BY

H. WHEELER ROBINSON
M.A., D.D.

PRINCIPAL OF REGENT'S PARK COLLEGE; PRESIDENT OF
THE BAPTIST HISTORICAL SOCIETY

LONDON:
THE KINGSGATE PRESS
4, SOUTHAMPTON ROW, W.C.1
1946

THE LIFE AND FAITH OF THE BAPTISTS

First Published in 1927
Revised Edition, 1946
Reprinted 1985

ISBN 0-913029-09-2

Chanticleer Publishing Company, Inc.
Box 501
Wake Forest, North Carolina 27587

PREFACE TO FIRST EDITION

IN this book I have tried to do two things at once, and therefore may have failed to do either adequately. One aim has been to describe the life and faith of the English Baptists in a way that will be intelligible to sympathetic readers of other communions. This means that I have tried throughout to state Baptist convictions as a particular form of the consciousness of the Catholic Church; I should not remain a Baptist if those convictions were not for me the doorway into the larger fellowship of all who are loyal to Jesus Christ. On the other hand, I have also thought of Baptist readers who might benefit by the exposition of their own faith and practice, especially in its underlying principles, as well as by frank criticism of its limitations. Neither aim follows the methods of propaganda, which are apt to exaggerate difference and to conceal weakness; but truth, as a man honestly sees it, is always in the long run the best *apologia*. If there are some things in the book which the "average" Baptist may not like, he must regard them as an illustration of that individualism which characterizes the Baptists perhaps more than any denomination, and supplies the chief elements of both their strength and their weakness. Perhaps I may best put myself right with him by appropriating the reply of Dr. Chandler to a prelate who asked him why he did not leave the Dissenters, since he admitted that certain things amongst them were unsatisfactory: "My Lord, I would, if I could find a worthier body of people."[1]

It is easy for the outsider to see the weakness of any system of religion and to miss the strength; it is possible for the insider to know the strength and to be unconscious of the weakness. Every type of religion will eventually be judged by its efficiency in mediating the fellowship of God and man; *securus judicat orbis terrarum*. It does not follow that what is best for one man is best for another; that at least must be admitted by all who give individualism its full place in religion. But no man knows what a particular type of

[1] Stoughton, *Religion in England under Queen Anne and the Georges*, i, p. 332.

religion can do for him until he has given himself wholeheartedly to it ; when he does, he discovers that fine paradox of ecclesiastical life, that catholicity is measured by depth of conviction, not by breadth of opinion. One truth boldly proclaimed was enough to make an Old Testament prophet ;[1] one truth held with sufficient intensity may bring a man into the circle of catholic Christianity, where he will find many other truths to learn.[2] But such a man must not be deterred by the imperfections of the Church and the faults of its members, existent under every system. If he looks for them he will easily find them, for the words "Seek and ye shall find" apply to evil as well as to good. The more difficult search for the good beneath the evil will discover the strength of religion within its apparent weakness. The simpler the system the more obvious the weakness, for an elaborate ritual and organization is better fitted to conceal the faults of our common humanity.

The plan of the book is somewhat unusual, but it has been deliberately chosen to give that emphasis of presentation which does more to create atmosphere than any particular thing that is said. After a brief statement of Baptist beginnings, and a characterization of the general spirit of the Baptists, a number of more or less typical figures or scenes from the seventeenth and eighteenth centuries are employed to bring out some features of Baptist life in concrete form. (These studies are purposely based, for the most part, on manuscript sources or rare books, not easily accessible.) These have not been continued into the nineteenth century, partly on grounds of space and partly because many assimilative influences were then bringing the different types of the Christian faith nearer to each other. Justification for the study of individuals, rather than of corporate history, may be found in the emphasis on individual experience which characterizes the Baptist faith and finds expression in the retention of the baptism of believers only (Chapter III).

[1] Cf. Robertson Smith, *The Prophets of Israel*, p. 182.
[2] If it be said that he may here find other truths more central than that with which he started, and logically calling for adhesion to another type of religion, then the certain loss through detachment from the old must be weighed against the possible gain from attachment to the new. But ever where conviction demands and obtains a new ecclesiastical life, gratitude for the service rendered by the old ought to remain.

From this follows the Baptist conception of the Church, as a fellowship of believers expressing that fellowship in worship and especially in the communion of the Lord's Supper, and nurturing it through specialized forms of that Christian "ministry" which is in itself incumbent on all (Chapter IV). It is further claimed that Baptists are conspicuous for two marked characteristics—their missionary spirit and their passion for liberty (Chapters V and VI). Finally, an attempt is made to estimate the value of their contribution to the Universal Church and their limitations (Chapter VII).

Several friends, to whom I am grateful, have helped me with criticisms and useful suggestions. My colleague, Professor A. J. D. Farrer, has read through the whole in typescript. Dr. W. T. Whitley, our leading authority on Baptist history (to whose book, *A History of British Baptists*, there is frequent indebtedness), has read the historical portions. The chapters dealing with Believers' Baptism and the Church have been read by the Rev. M. E. Aubrey, secretary of the Baptist Union. The chapter dealing with missionary work has been read by the Revs. C. E. Wilson and W. Y. Fullerton, secretaries of the Baptist Missionary Society. I have to thank the editors of *The Review and Expositor* (Louisville, U.S.A.), *The Baptist Quarterly*, and *The Baptist Times* for permission to make use of some material which has already appeared in their pages.

H. WHEELER ROBINSON.

REGENT'S PARK COLLEGE.

PREFACE TO SECOND EDITION

THE first edition of this book was published in 1927 by Messrs. Methuen and Co., Ltd., in their series "The Faiths: Varieties of Christian Expression", and is now out of print. The publisher's share of the copyright has been transferred to the Kingsgate Press, and I have to thank Messrs. Methuen and Co. for their courteous consent to this transfer. The opportunity has been taken to revise the text in a few small details, to bring the statistical information up to date and to add a short concluding chapter on "The Final Authority". I have to thank my former colleague, the Rev. A. J. D. Farrer, for the renewal of the help which he gave to the first edition, and Dr. J. H. Rushbrooke for providing me with the latest figures regarding Baptists throughout the world. I owe a very special debt to the Rev. E. A. Payne, who has not only made many useful suggestions, most of which I have adopted, but has also put me under deep obligation by preparing the bibliography, which is a new feature, and by seeing this second edition through the press at a time when illness has prevented me from incurring sole responsibility for this.*

H. WHEELER ROBINSON.

OXFORD, MARCH, 1945.

---

* Dr. Wheeler Robinson completed his notes for this new edition and drafted the above preface only a few weeks before his death which took place on May 12th, 1945. Care has been taken to make only such changes in the text as he had explicitly approved. The concluding chapter of which he speaks has been put as an appendix.
—E.A.P.

CONTENTS

		PAGE
PREFACE TO FIRST EDITION		v
PREFACE TO SECOND EDITION		viii

I. THE ORIGIN AND PRINCIPLES OF THE BAPTISTS . . 11

II. STUDIES IN BAPTIST PERSONALITY 25
    (1) A Baptist Home (Caleb Vernon) . . . 25
    (2) A Baptist Soldier (William Allen) . . . 32
    (3) A Baptist Reformer (Thomas Lambe) . . 36
    (4) A Baptist Teacher (Benjamin Keach) . . 38
    (5) A Baptist Church (Cripplegate) 41
        (*a*) Discipline 42
        (*b*) Hymn-singing 48
    (6) A Baptist Writer (Ann Dutton) . . . 50
    (7) A Baptist Student (John Collett Ryland) . . 56
    (8) A Baptist Preacher (Robert Hall) . . . 65

III. BELIEVERS' BAPTISM AND THE EMPHASIS ON INDIVIDUAL EXPERIENCE 69
    (1) The Meaning and Justification of Believers' Baptism 69
    (2) The Importance of Conversion 74
    (3) The Confessional Value of Believers' Baptism . 77

IV. THE BAPTIST DOCTRINE OF THE CHURCH . . . 82
    (1) Membership and Polity 82
    (2) Worship 93
    (3) The Communion of the Lord's Supper . . 97
    (4) Ministry 102

V. THE MISSIONARY SPIRIT OF THE BAPTISTS . . . 108

		PAGE
VI.	THE PASSION OF THE BAPTISTS FOR LIBERTY	123
VII.	THE STRENGTH AND THE WEAKNESS OF THE BAPTISTS	139

APPENDICES :

    I.—The Final Authority 148
    II.—Selected Bibliography 152
    III.—World Statistics 154

INDEX :

    I.—Persons 155
    II.—Subjects 157

ERRATA

Page 37, line 26, *for* " trough " *read* " through ".

Page 57, line 10, *for* " wears " *read* " years ".

Page 132, line 8, should read " Preachers were required to subscribe the Anglican articles ".

Page 143, line 10, *for* " that " *read* " than ".

Page 148, line 1 of footnote, *for* " addition " *read* " edition ".

Page 152, line 19, *for* " (1946) " *read* " (1947) ".

Page 153, line 8, *for* " the last named " *read* " E. A. Payne ".

Page 153, *insert* between lines 9 and 10 " History—*The Free Church Tradition in the Life of England* ".

THE LIFE AND FAITH OF THE BAPTISTS

I

THE ORIGIN AND PRINCIPLES OF THE BAPTISTS

A CANDID inquirer from another planet, visiting this earth for the first time, might well be perplexed at the apparent multitude of differing religions in England. "I find half a dozen varieties", he might say, "in a single street; how am I to know which is right, and is it not far more likely that they are all wrong? If they were working on right lines, surely by this time they would have reached a unity in the truth far more important than their diversity in the expression of it." As a matter of fact, if our Martian took the trouble to attend the half-dozen Free Churches he might have found in the street he would realize that they *had* reached a practical unity, regardless of their notice-boards, and that the prayer and the praise and the preaching were largely indistinguishable by their denominational brand. On the other hand, if he drew the hasty inference that the differences between the Free Churches were therefore negligible, because not very apparent to the superficial observer, he would be quite wrong. Though they all belong to the Protestant, and for the most part to the Puritan, tradition of the Church, they represent different emphases, and have made different contributions to the Church and to the Kingdom of God. They all carry on the witness of the Reformation, but they do it with varieties of accent and expression that are by no means to be ignored. That witness is "the new conception of the relation of the individual soul to God, which found expression in [Luther's] distinctive doctrine of justification by faith".[1] Then, as now, there were many contributory forces, such as the rise of nationalism, with its challenge of ecclesiastical imperialism; the new learning, with its criticism of mediæval claims; the consciousness of economic oppression, with its

[1] James Mackinnon, *Luther and the Reformation*, i, p. v.

revolt against the feudal system. But the central force was undoubtedly that which found its expression through Luther —the religious individualism which has been working out its consequences, for good and for evil, ever since. Of that individualism, the Baptists might fairly claim to be the extreme representatives, the very lance-head of the Reformation impact. The name they bear, which is the label affixed by others, calls attention to the fact that they retain the New Testament rite of baptism for the individual response of faith to the Gospel, and have not extended this rite, like other Churches, to those who are yet unconscious of the meaning of individual responsibility. That name, in the form of Anabaptist, or "re-baptizer", was first given to the far-reaching and multi-coloured continental movement, which extended over Europe in the sixteenth century, and in some quarters issued in shameful excesses.[1] But though there are some points of possible contact between this movement in its more moderate forms and those Englishmen who became Baptists, whether in Holland or in England, the origin of English Baptists is to be found rather in their Puritan ancestry.[2] In history, as well as in idea, the Baptists carry forward the idea of the Reformation to its furthest issue, and have not unfairly been described as "Protestant of the Protestants".[3]

This direct line of development is admirably illustrated in John Smyth, the first English Baptist, who occupies a place similar to that of Robert Browne amongst the Congregationalists, though unlike Browne he did not ultimately abandon his distinctive form of Church polity. Smyth was a Cambridge scholar who became the Puritan chaplain (as we should

---

[1] A brief account of the Anabaptist movement is given in my *Baptist Principles*, pp. 59-64. Further details will be found in Lindsay's *History of the Reformation*, ii, pp. 430 ff., or A. H. Newman's *History of Anti-Pedobaptism*.

[2] See the *Baptist Quarterly*, January, 1924, "Continental Anabaptists and Early English Baptists;" by W. T. Whitley and A. J. D. Farrer; the chapter on "The Anabaptists in England before 1612" in *The Early English Dissenters*, by Champlin Burrage; the *Transactions of the Congregational Historical Society*, vols. xii and xiii, articles by D. B. Heriot; and R. J. Smithson, *The Anabaptists*, 1935. There is an explicit disclaimer of the name "Anabaptist" by John Murton in 1615 (see *Tracts on Liberty of Conscience*, Hanserd Knollys edition, p. 179).

[3] J. H. Rushbrooke in the collection of addresses by himself and others called *The Faith of the Baptists* (Kingsgate Press, 1926).

ORIGIN AND PRINCIPLES OF BAPTISTS

say) to the city of Lincoln, at the beginning of the seventeenth century. As a Puritan, he was still an Anglican, eager for the further reform of the Anglican Church, and working from within it to this end. Some years later he removed to Gainsborough, and after a protracted struggle decided that he must withdraw from the Anglican communion to realize his idea of the Church—that is, he became a Separatist. If he had remained at this stage of development his name would have been added to the list of Congregationalist pioneers, for it was the Congregationalist type of Church polity which his Church illustrated. Over against the parochial idea of the Church he and his comrades set that of a group of converted men, who had consciously based their fellowship on a covenant. John Smyth's covenant was remarkable because it pledged these Separatists " to walk in all His (Christ's) ways made known, or to be made known unto them, according to their best endeavours, whatsoever it should cost them ". They were ready to believe that " the Lord had more light and truth yet to break forth out of His holy Word ". As a matter of fact, John Robinson, who gave this better-known saying to the world, was a friend and assistant to John Smyth before they both went to Holland in search of freedom to worship God, and seems to have derived the great principle from him. In Amsterdam John Smyth obeyed his own Church Covenant by following the guidance of the New Testament into Baptist convictions; he was led to maintain in teaching and practice that the true basis of the Church was not an arbitrary covenant, but the ordinance of baptism administered to believers only. Some of his followers, led by Thomas Helwys, came over to London in 1611-12, and there founded the first Baptist Church in England. It should be noticed that the baptism they then practised was by pouring, not by immersion. The mode was a secondary matter; the primary truth was baptism as the basis of a regenerate Church—a Church, that is, according to the New Testament pattern and the Puritan ideal.[1] Anyone who thinks that Baptists then or now are primarily contending for the *mode* of immersion does not really know what their faith is. They stand for what they

---

[1] When the question of the mode was raised a generation later, it was speedily decided in favour of immersion, which has the advantages of New Testament support and eloquence of expression. See pp. 69f.

believe to be the logic of Separatist Puritanism, according to the example and practice of the New Testament. They refuse to obscure their testimony to the necessity for a converted Church by administering ·baptism to any but believers in Christ, whilst they are in sympathy with any expression of the responsibility of the Church for its young life which avoids this obscuration.

The Baptist movement begun by Smyth and Helwys issued in what came to be known as General Baptist Churches, viz. those which were Arminian in their theology, as contrasted with the prevailing Calvinism of contemporary Puritanism. But the main line of Baptist Church life moved along the lines of a Calvinistic theology, giving rise to what came to be known as Particular Baptist Churches, i.e. Churches holding the Calvinistic doctrine of election. According to this view (then prevalent in a great part of Protestantism), the Atonement was not made for all men, but only for those whom God had chosen for salvation ; it was particular and not " general ", i.e. universal. The first known Particular Baptist Church was also due to evolution from Congregational Separatism, like the first General Baptist Church. It arose in London between 1630 and 1640,[1] and here also baptism was at first by affusion or pouring, though immersion is prescribed as the true mode in the first Particular Baptist Confession, of date 1644. The General Baptists and the Particular Baptists have had separate histories ; the former have become negligible, the latter have gradually abandoned their original Calvinism, or at least its rigour. In 1770 there was a " New Connexion " formed amongst the more evangelical of the General Baptists which approximated to the main body, and in 1891 the distinction ceased to exist.

Baptist history now extends over three centuries, in the course of which they have become one of the largest Protestant denominations, with upwards of thirteen million communicants, chiefly in the United States of America.[2] In Great Britain and Ireland their communicant membership is nearly 400,000. In the seventeenth century they were prominent in the Puritan struggle for political and religious freedom, notably in Cromwell's army, though many of them

[1] See the chart given by J. H. Shakespeare in *Baptist and Congregational Pioneers*, pp. 184, 185.
[2] See Appendix III.

did not approve of the later developments in Cromwell's personal position and policy. In the eighteenth century they shared in the general lethargy of religion prior to the Evangelical Revival, but towards the close of the century they had the proud privilege of being pioneers in foreign missionary work, through William Carey. In the nineteenth century they carried on their twofold witness to the rights of conscience and the power of the Gospel through such men as are best represented by William Knibb and John Clifford on the one hand, and by Robert Hall, Alexander Maclaren, and Charles Haddon Spurgeon on the other. Now, in the twentieth century, they are facing those problems of corporate life which await every Church, however individualistic its origin and principle, and by voluntary effort have raised several great funds for the common welfare of Baptist Churches.

The Baptist contribution to the religious life of the nation during the last three centuries has not been spectacular, though it has had its great moments and has been very real. It has been less than it might have been, not only through the failure to maintain the high ideal of a regenerate Church, but also through the repression of Free Church life by ecclesiastical tyranny and political blindness, from which all the Free Churches have suffered in some degree. From that repression we have emerged slowly, and Baptists at any rate have not yet learnt to value the opportunities for larger education and the cultivation of the larger humanities as they ought.[1] But underneath the public life of the three centuries there has been flowing a steady stream of contribution to the common good —largely through humble homes and the conventicles of back streets.

Like all other Protestants, Baptists are thrown back on the Bible for the justification of their faith. It should never be overlooked that the English Reformation has its roots in the native soil, whatever it owed to the Lutheranism and the Calvinism of the Continent, and that this soil had been prepared by Wycliffe's work in making the Bible accessible. Thus Professor A. F. Pollard says: " The views of the English Reformers approach so much more nearly to those of Wycliffe

[1] See, however, the essay by E. A. Payne, "The Development of Nonconformist Theological Education in the Nineteenth Century with special reference to Regent's Park College" in *Studies in History and Religion* (Lutterworth Press, 1942).

than to those of Luther that the Englishman rather than the German must be regarded as the morning star of the Anglican Reformation." [1] T. M. Lindsay, in his general *History of the Reformation* (p. 316, vol. ii) points out that " Lollardy had never died out in England, and Lollardy was simply the English form of that passive protest against the mediæval Church which under various names had maintained itself in France, Germany, and Bohemia for centuries in spite of persecution ". [2] To the same effect writes G. M. Trevelyan in his *History of England*: —

Every important aspect of the English Reformation was of native origin. All can be traced back as far as Wycliffe, and some much farther. . . . A generation before Luther sprang to sudden fame, Lollardy, long suppressed, had come into the open once more. It was native to the soil of England, and had been faithfully preserved in cottage and workshop as a poor man's tradition by the spiritual ancestors of John Bunyan (pp. 250, 289).

John Bunyan and his fellow-Baptists had a special and distinctive reason for the appeal to Scripture. It was their one ground for the practice of believers' baptism which could be maintained against the appeal to the tradition of the Church. Now that constant appeal to Scripture for the distinctive denominational testimony, which is found with what many will think wearisome iteration, has had an important result. It has helped to make and keep Baptists a Bible-loving Church. The baptism of believers by immersion has not only emphasized conscious faith as essential to the Church, but it has also, by its symbolism, constantly recalled men to the foundation of the Gospel in history, the death and the resurrection of Jesus Christ, which, as Paul argued, are represented in the act of the believer's immersion and his rising from the waters of baptism. That act, constantly repeated before the eyes of Baptists, has taken the place of any formal creed, and helped to keep them an evangelical Church, without any authoritative confession of faith. Like the Lord's Supper, it has preached the Lord's death until He come, whilst leaving believers free, in successive generations, to interpret

[1] *Thomas Cranmer and the English Reformation*, 1906, p. 90.
[2] Hastings Rashdall, in the *Dictionary of National Biography*, s.v. " Wycliffe," p. 1133: " It may be broadly asserted that lollardy never quite died out in England till it merged in the new Lutheran heresies of the sixteenth century."

afresh the meaning of that redemptive death. Such liberty within loyalty is in the true succession of the religion of the Bible, which extended over a thousand years, and shows many changes of development, along with a true unity of growth.

This, of course, raises an important issue for the present day. Has not the criticism of the Bible, by which is meant not scepticism or unbelief, but the interpretation of Scripture in the light of all knowledge, and without any pre-conceived theory—has not the criticism of the Bible cut the ground away from beneath the feet of Baptists? Is it not out of date to insist on a Biblical rite at all?

This is not, of course, the place to attempt any adequate discussion of the modern attitude to the Bible in relation to evangelical belief in general. But the spread of education amongst Baptists as amongst other communities is bound to raise the issue of the nature of the authority which it is rightly felt must somehow be exercised by the Bible. On the lowest view, the Bible is the classic of Christian experience, and as such claims a permanent place and power in shaping the belief and practice of successive generations. Without it, as history has shown, the Church is apt to become an official institution, and individual experience is apt to lose its way in mere subjectivities. Whatever may be thought of the horizon and methods of "Fundamentalism",[1] there can be no doubt that a true principle is embedded in the errors and prejudices of the movement. That principle is the reality of an "objective"

---

[1] We find a good deal of literalistic interpretation in the course of Baptist history, and a good deal of conservatism in this respect amongst Baptists at the present time, especially in America. This literalistic interpretation became politically important in the time of the Commonwealth. The "Fifth Monarchy" movement, in which Baptists were prominent, applied the apocalyptic visions of Daniel to contemporary events. After the monarchies of the four "beasts", there was to be a fifth monarchy of the saints of the Most High (Dan. vii. 27). "The politics of seven years from 1653 were influenced gravely by this party" (Whitley, *History of British Baptists*, p. 85). They had previously desired the removal of Charles; they opposed the "kingship" of Cromwell. The movement culminated under Thomas Venner (not himself a Baptist) in the insurrection of 1660-61, after which, as Dr. Whitley points out, "the millenarian tinge faded out; but the literalistic temper remained, and attention being attracted to the fourth commandment, the Fifth-Monarchists transformed into Seventh-day Baptists". These have had but a negligible existence in this country, and now hardly survive; but in the United States the movement is still of some importance.

revelation of some kind to educate and to confirm the "subjective" experience of God, the necessity for a record of collective experience to guide and control the religious growth of the individual. We go astray only when we lay down beforehand the kind of revelation the Bible ought to be. The unprejudiced student will find that it is a "source-book" rather than a textbook of faith and practice. But to admit this is not to be deprived of the Bible as authoritative; it is only to be driven back to the intrinsic evidence of God in human experience as recorded in the Bible. Behind the literature of the book there is the life that inspired it. If God spoke through the prophets and supremely in the Son, there will be evidence of His truth in the testimony itself. This throws us back on the Reformation principle of the *Testimonium Spiritus Sancti Internum*—the witness of the Spirit of God with our spirits.[1] This is not a phrase to conceal a weakness. The emphasis on the Spirit of God—that is, on the activity of His real presence in the inner and outer experience of men—has characterized the Christian faith from the beginning. The prophecy may be ventured that amongst the Baptists in particular there will be a growing recognition of this relatively neglected truth—a recognition to which they are already committed by their insistence on baptism in the New Testament sense. Baptism signifies the entrance into a life of fellowship with Christ, which means a baptism of the Holy Spirit.

If Baptists had contended for a rite without any central and permanent meaning, they would never have grown as they have. There must have been a deep appeal behind the rite, a central truth of permanent importance—as, indeed, practically all Churches virtually maintain by their retention of Baptism in some form or meaning. A baptism of *faith* takes us into the very centre of Christian experience, and is no bit of antiquated folk-lore. Further, the critical study of the Bible serves only the more to bring out the historical development of faith, and to show the emergence in the Bible history of those very contentions about the Church for which Baptists, along with other Free Churchmen, are standing. These are chiefly three, and I can do no more here than briefly indicate them.

---

[1] See my essay on "The Validity of Christian Experience" in the volume called *The Future of Christianity* (ed. by Marchant), reprinted and developed in *Redemption and Revelation* (1942).

First of all, there is the right of the soul to an immediate relation to God—the right which was reasserted in the Reformation by the doctrine of the universal priesthood of believers. In the earlier days of Israel there were many practices and beliefs, which we should call superstitions, coming between the soul and God.[1] In the latter, post-exilic, history of Judaism there was an elaborate priesthood which mediated God to men and men to God. But in the centre of the Old Testament development, as modern historical study has brought out clearly, there were the prophets and the prophetic consciousness. That consciousness asserts that God could put aside all barriers and limits erected by human hands and reveal Himself to men, as directly as, or even more directly than, in the ways of simple human fellowship, and that man could approach God with the same simplicity and directness. That is the core of the Old Testament religion, and the Christian consciousness of the New Testament follows on in that succession, under the guidance of the Prophet of Nazareth. Elaborate ways of worshipping God are described in the Bible, but the line of living development traceable through a thousand years is one of great simplicity. The truth which dawned upon the first believers was as startling as the dawn of day could be to eyes that saw it for the first time: "Our fellowship is with the Father and with His Son, Jesus Christ." Any human priesthood is apt to seem an irrelevance, if not an impertinence, for those who have once experienced that fellowship in its direct simplicity.

Second, there is the fact, also illustrated by the great prophets and continued in the apostles and disciples of New Testament times, that the chief content of this fellowship is moral holiness, that the believers are called to be saints, consecrated to the holy God by moral character. This was the vehicle of the Old Testament revelation through the prophets and the essence of the substance of that revelation. The plain duty of man to man was the highest offering man could bring to the God who desired mercy and not sacrifice. Without holiness no man can see God, but the pure in heart shall see Him. This inward and ethical emphasis stands in contrast with the externalism of the older idolatry and the later legalism.

Third, there is the principle of the regenerate Church

[1] E.g. the breach of taboo seen in Uzzah's death (2 Sam. vi. 6, 7), or the theory of the origin of circumcision given in Exod. iv. 24-6.

already to be found in the Old Testament before it was asserted in the New. Down from the times of Isaiah, who committed his testimony to his disciples, when the mass of his fellow-countrymen rejected it, we may trace this "little Church within the Church" of the nation on to the New Testament times.[1] In the dark days of Manasseh there were disciples of the prophets to whom we owe our Book of Deuteronomy, and the Reformation under Josiah. In the exile of Babylon there was a living nucleus, for which the latter part of the Book of Isaiah was written. In the fifth century those who feared the Lord spoke one to another, and formed a little Church. We see that Church in and behind many of the Psalms. We note its heroic revival and witness in the time of the Maccabees. It was to the successors of that long and faithful line that Jesus and His disciples appealed to fashion the new Israel. It was vital to the prophetic message to create such a community within the nation, for what whole nation has ever been a true Church? For that principle we stand to-day when we assert that the ideal of the Church must always be the community of the regenerate, a principle which is the life-breath of the Free Churches and is most emphatically expressed by the faith and practice of believers' baptism. May we not say, then, that critical study of the Bible, which has brought out these principles in their historical development so much more clearly than when the more priestly elements of the Old Testament were thought to be primary, has not weakened, but strengthened, the Baptist witness? We cannot, it is true, use the Bible to-day as Bunyan used it in *Grace Abounding*—as a body of oracles to be applied directly to life without any regard to the content of its truths. We are not likely to see in the Bible just what he did—a dramatic commentary on our own lives in all their personal details. But if we have lost the power of doing this, God has given us in the new knowledge of Scripture a more than adequate recompense. He has shown us that the Free Churches belong to a great historical development, with a nobler and more ancient lineage than even the Roman Church can claim.[2]

[1] See *The Cross of the Servant*, by H. Wheeler Robinson, p. 38, and cf. Isa. viii. 16, which suggests "an important epoch in the history of religion—the emergence of a spiritual, as distinct from a national, religious society" (Buchanan Gray, *Isaiah*, p. 155).

[2] See E. A. Payne, *The Free Church Tradition in the Life of England*, 1944, and *The Fellowship of Believers*, 1944.

But the real objection most men to-day might bring against the conception of the Church as the community of the regenerate (i.e. those who have experienced repentance and faith, which is what we mean by Christian conversion) is not that it is wrong, but that it is impracticable. "A beautiful theory," someone will say, "but is it really found in practice to be true?" Are the Churches which most emphasize the necessity for a regenerate membership conspicuously better than other Churches? Is it not as well frankly to recognize the limitations of human nature, and be content with a fair average, and to shape the polity of the Church simply by what is practically expedient? That is a line of argument which peculiarly appeals to Englishmen, who distrust ideas and love a practical policy. There is a good deal of truth in it, and we must not deny that truth. A wide gap separates the ideal of the regenerate Church from its actual practice. Discipline is now reserved almost only for those grosser sins which would create public scandal. The young believer often receives a shock of disillusionment as he comes to realize, quickly or gradually, how different the real of Church life amongst us is from the ideal. Would any of us venture to describe the particular Church he knows most intimately as made up of living temples of the Holy Spirit? Is there not a great appeal in the Catholic conception of the Church as a parochial Noah's Ark, a paternal gathering of those who are to be saved, rather than a select company of the saved?

Let us frankly admit the truth of this. Any Church we know is made up of men of like passions with ourselves, men for whom the saintly life is an ideal rather than the real. There are some in it struggling in the grip of passions, from the tyranny of which they have not yet wholly escaped, though they are striving to get out of the Slough of Despond on the right side, and though they struggle to their feet in the Valley of Humiliation wounded but fighting still. There are men with unconscious inconsistencies and weaknesses, men to whom the Parable of the Sower has an individual application, for in them there are tracts of ground on which the seed lies exposed, or on which the thorns grow, or where the soil is very thin. There are differences of taste that may annoy us more than these moral inconsistencies, differences of thought and expression that perplex us, genuine differences of conviction even within the same Church which it seems impossible to reconcile with our own. What shall we make of all these things in the light of the theory that the Church is the Body of Christ indwelt by the Holy Spirit of God?

This—that from the very beginning of God's work in the world He has worked in some sort of disguise. He hides Himself in Nature, so that He often seems cruel and relentless there. He hides Himself in grace, so that we still have to discover the Eternal Son of God in the guise of a Jewish peasant. He hides Himself in the Church, so that the real presence and activity of the Holy Spirit in the individual and in the society is not always or easily apparent. God the Holy Spirit accepts the limitations of human lives, even those of their moral imperfection, and works out His purpose in this mingled texture, wherein the golden thread of the pattern must be sought out. There must be personal faith, for it is by the hearing of faith that the Holy Spirit is received.[1] But faith does not ensure infallibility, intellectual or moral.

The Free Churches stand or fall by the doctrine of the Holy Spirit, as every kind of true Church must do. But in proportion to the simplicity of their worship and ecclesiastical machinery they offer themselves the more to criticism, and show the more plainly the contrast between theory and practice which is found in all men and in all Churches. If we bring the ideal and the real sharply together, we make our failures the more evident. It is easy enough with an elaborate machinery of officialdom, an elaborate ritual of pomp and power, to shift the emphasis from the human company to some remote and hardly visible entity. The red-robed cardinals of the Vatican are far enough away for *their* weaknesses to be unknown. The sonorous Latin of the Mass produces an emotional effect without any effort of intelligent thought, and has the dignity of ancient generations. Substitute a little company of villagers met for prayer in some ugly little chapel, and it is much easier to criticize the realization of a New Testament Church of saints. Yet are men to be slaves of their imagination? Is truth to depend on the mere picturesqueness of its expression? The ultimate issue is the same for all the Churches, and it is finely expressed by the words in which Alice Meynell bids us see in the communicant brother kneeling at our side the Real Presence of Christ, who speaks to us from that unknown heart

[1] Gal. iii. 2.

> . . . in all his strife,
> All his felicity, his good and ill,
> In the assaulted stronghold of his will,
>
> I do confess Thee here,
> Alive within this life; I know Thee near
> Within this lonely conscience, closed away
> Within this brother's solitary day.[1]

All this does not mean that any one form of Church polity is to be regarded as divinely ordained and prescribed for all time. The similar polity of Baptists and Congregationalists is open to improvement in many ways, and must be modified to meet new needs. It has learnt, and is learning, from both Methodism and Presbyterianism, and will doubtless learn more in the future, for we each of us have something to teach the rest. But this does not alter the fact that the Churches which present the ideal in closest and simplest contact with the real of life must expect to meet the sharpest criticism in their attempt to maintain the ideal. A. M. Fairbairn stated that ideal thus, in its four determinative elements:—

> A church is (a) a society of the godly, or of men who truly believe and piously live. (b) It is a society instituted expressly to realize in the personal and collective life the religious ideals of Christ. (c) It is capable of extension only by means that produce faith, and of development only by agencies that create godliness. (d) It is autonomous and authoritative, possessed of the freedom necessary to the fulfilment of its mission, the realization of its ideals; and it is endowed with all the legislative and administrative powers needed for the maintenance of order and the attainment of progress (*Studies in Religion and Theology*, p. 215).

We may not argue for that ideal in quite the old way, by setting the examples of Scripture as authoritative precedents against the traditions of the Church. The modern appeal will be increasingly to the ultimate authority of experience—that Christian experience which both Scripture and Church express. But the appeal to experience need not dismay us, for it is the inner logic of the Reformation itself. In the long run it is the appeal to experience which will settle the argument, as it always does. We may serve the truth more by persistence in the ideal, whilst not concealing our present

---

[1] "The Unknown God" (*Oxford Book of Mystical Verse*, p. 462).

failure to realize it, than by sacrificing part of that ideal in the interests of expediency.

It may be convenient to summarize what has been said about Baptist principles in this chapter by quoting the statement of a leading American Baptist.[1] The angle of approach is naturally somewhat different, and we may find it necessary to make some modification of emphasis later on, but most Baptists would accept this as a fair statement of their position:—

The Biblical significance of the Baptists is the right of private interpretation [of], and obedience to, the Scriptures. The significance of the Baptists in relation to the individual is soul freedom. The ecclesiastical significance of the Baptists is a regenerated church-membership and the equality and priesthood of believers. The political significance of the Baptists is the separation of Church and State. But as comprehending all the above particulars, as a great and aggressive force in Christian history, as distinguished from all others and standing entirely alone, the doctrine of the soul's competency in religion under God is the distinctive significance of the Baptists.

[1] E. Y. Mullins, *The Axioms of Religion*, pp. 56, 57.

II

STUDIES IN BAPTIST PERSONALITY

THE aim of these brief studies is to give an inside view of Baptists as they thought and lived in the seventeenth and eighteenth centuries—Baptists in their weakness as well as in their strength, and in the unconscious humour of their ways, as well as in their abiding convictions. It would have been easy to make a much more impressive selection of names, e.g. to substitute John Foster the essayist, one of the few Baptist writers of real literary distinction, for the unknown Ann Dutton, who has no claim to be remembered except as a "type". Moreover, two more names at least should have been added to show the thought and life of the nineteenth century, viz. those of Charles Haddon Spurgeon and John Clifford, so different and yet so complementary. But these are well known, and their lives can be studied in full-length biographies.[1] If these two be added mentally to this chapter, the reader will have a fair view, within the limits of space, of the course of the three Baptist centuries, more illuminative in its detail than any condensed consecutive history could be.[2] It is indeed characteristic of the Baptist faith that its emphasis should thus fall on the creation of personality in its individualism. Readers of other communions will perhaps think it chiefly wanting on the other side of personality—viz. sociality—at least so far as *formal* expression in organization and corporate emphasis is concerned. But voluntary co-operation has its own advantages.

(1) A BAPTIST HOME (CALEB VERNON)

On a late summer's day of the Plague Year, just when Samuel Pepys was publicly debating how to cope with it, and privately hesitating to wear his new periwig, "because the

---

[1] *C. H. Spurgeon*, by W. Y. Fullerton (1920); *Dr. John Clifford*, by Sir James Marchant (1924).
[2] The studies are more or less linked together by the people who emerge in them.

plague was in Westminster when I bought it", you might have seen a boat rowed down the Thames, with a consumptive boy of twelve lying in it. Even so short a journey as that from the pleasant country resort known as Battersea to the London of two and a half centuries ago had its perils; it proved that both the waterman who rowed the boat and the servant who carried the light weight of Caleb Vernon from the river to his father's lodging were sickening for death by the pestilence. But the emaciated frame held a dominating purpose; he would not be away from his father nor take his father away from his physician's work; he wanted to sympathize with the sufferings of the Lord's poor visited people by being with them; above all, there was a burning passion for the religious fellowship with which the garden-house at Battersea could not provide him. The story of this gifted and precocious life of twelve and a half years has been told by the father in a little book of great interest called *The Compleat Scholler* (1666).[1] This is the book which gives us incidentally so vivid a glimpse of a Baptist home in the seventeenth century.

Let us get to know this home at one of its most characteristic moments, that of family prayers. It is the first occasion after the boy's return, and the Scripture lesson is taken from the ninth chapter of Ecclesiastes. The father dwells very impressively on the tenth verse, and enforces its application: "Whatsoever thy hand findeth to do, do it with thy might; for there is no work, nor device, nor knowledge, nor wisdom in the grave whither thou goest." It is not perhaps the point *we* should choose for the edification of a sick child, but those were more Spartan days. The father himself is an old cavalry general, who once knew and wrote about horses, and has now, as a physician, transferred his knowledge to dealing with men. He has known intimately the richly varied life of the seventeenth century; has been awakened from conventional religion to that passion for reality which such men as Gifford could kindle; has fought the heresies of Quakerism and the presumptions of the Protector; has tried in vain to establish a new constitution, when the Cromwell family disappointed hope; now calmly continues to preach and to heal, though he has known what Newgate

[1] Two copies only are known to exist—one in the Bodleian and the other in the Angus Library of Regent's Park College.

meant, and warrants have long been out for his arrest, in these disappointing Restoration days. Side by side with John Vernon is the wife he won from Devonshire in those great days of the forties, when he and William Allen were officers in the army of Fairfax and married sisters. Perhaps Uncle William looks in sometimes and tells of the Windsor Prayer Meeting, which decided to call Charles Stuart, that man of blood, to account for the blood he had shed. Another visitor of gentler spirit is Abraham Cheare, ready to repeat to the children some of his last-written verses. Besides Caleb, there are his brother and three younger sisters, Mary of seven, Betty of five, and Nancy still younger. Nor must we forget Honour, the maid, who has brought Caleb up from the cradle and taught him till he began Latin. For this is not a home that makes piety a protection of ignorance. Caleb at four could read the Bible, and at six was apt in doctrine and practice ; at seven he went to school, at ten had begun to add Greek to his Latin, and found time for some Hebrew. But Caleb has already felt the clash between his classical authors and the teaching of his Bible ; he has already shown a remarkable religious development, very real in itself, though the forms of its expression will seem artificial and overstrained to us. At ten Caleb wrote a letter about religion to an older friend, which raised grave doubts in the reader's mind as to its authenticity. He replied with severe kindness. " I received thine without date, but not without serious desire of the best things ", and went on to catechize him as to some of the terms used, such as " an outside professor ", from which catechism Caleb emerged with reasonable success.

We get another glimpse of this family as they sit round the table and the father calls on this or that child to say grace. The Puritans took their " grace " seriously. Do we not remember that Roger Williams argued that an unregenerate child ought not to be allowed to say grace, whereupon an opponent retorted that since the thankless reception of God's gifts was certainly wrong, an unregenerate child should be given no food at all? Here it is Caleb who overcomes his natural timidity and (repenting of a previous refusal) comes forward to encourage the others by his example. Caleb's relations with his little sisters are tender and natural. He gives them his toys towards the end of his short life ; it is good to know that there were toys in this grave religious home. When they were in the country, Nancy, aged five, would say to Honour, the maid, in the morning, " What mercy is it we are alive, and so many thousands taken away at London, and so many little children! " whilst Caleb says to Nancy as she sits by his bed, surely a demure and grave little nurse: " Nancy, the Lord make you a mother in Israel. Oh, how I long to see Christ formed in you!" But the old Adam is still in Nancy, for whilst Caleb lies ill, her childish voice rings up to the room, " Who shall have Caleb's bird when he is dead? " Caleb's sense of justice is seen in the fact that he instantly awards the bird, if he dies, to the younger Betty, because Nancy has one already. Caleb has a keen sense of justice. In one of his bad times, the noise of his little sisters and their cousin was more than he could bear, and he quoted Job at them: "To him that is in affliction pity should be showed by his friends ". But he is soon sorry for this feeling of annoyance, and calls the children that he may cut them out some of his special jelly. The worst sins Caleb can remember are that once he disobeyed his mother by not going to bed when she had commanded it, and that " he had spent his time very childishly, and plaid away his convictions". We think of Augustine's stolen pears and Bunyan's tip-cat. But Nature has ingenious ways of thrusting in when we have thrust her out. Towards the end, when Caleb was very weak, " he desired some living creature might stand on the bed by him to prevent Melancholly thoughts, when he could not rest: being asked, what? He said a young Lamb, Pigeon, Rabbit or anything, but a Squerril being named (hoping it might easily be procured), he was earnest for that, having, he said, never seen any but once in the field ". The squirrel could not be got, and the boy was much disappointed, for, as he told his father, " I find myself inclining to melancholy, and I think such a thing would be pretty company for me, and therein I may see the workmanship of God ". One great though transitory temptation came to him in his sore pain—to curse God and die ; the intensity of his thought about it reminds us of Bunyan's " Sell Him! " But we must admit that there is something a little unnatural when a boy of ten desires to weep over the sins of his youthful days! It tempts us to say, though in this instance at least we should be wrong, that such repetition of phrases means no more than the curses which little children pick up with equal facility.

The central event in these simple annals of a Baptist home is Caleb's desire to be baptized—a desire to which his father and friends are all opposed because of the serious character of his illness. There is something both admirable and, pathetic in the way this sick boy fights for his conviction that he ought to be baptized, yet bows reluctantly to the right of others to say the last word. A representative meeting of the Church, numbering twenty persons, is held in his bedroom, candles being set on the bed, and they round about him, whilst this singular child begins his testimony, "God spake once, yea twice, yet man regardeth it not", and proceeds to apply this to two previous illnesses. He confesses that his great sin is to have been "frothy". He is carefully cross-examined on the faith—for example, on the priestly, kingly and prophetic offices of Christ—and he gives his reasons for desiring baptism, which are especially the words "He that believeth and is baptized shall be saved"; the example of Christ, Philip and the eunuch, "If thou believest with all thy heart, thou mayest", and the case of the jailer. He is warned of the physical danger in his case, but is quite undeterred. It is of interest to notice the close contact of the home and the Church in the way the father deals with his own perplexity as to allowing this baptism. He holds a prayer-meeting with others about it, "with prayer setting forth his great strait in the case ; and taking their answer one by one, upon what they had heard, both for and against it". Finally, the father decided to trust God with the issue. But even then a physician friend came between the child's eager desire and its satisfaction, pointing out the danger and the scandal, and declaring that Caleb could not be carried alive to the place of baptism. This friend is brought in to argue with poor Caleb, and makes use of a very unfair bit of exegesis: "It was said, all Judæa *went* out to be baptized, but he never heard that any were *carried* out." I am glad poor Caleb had the wit to reply: "Christ bid his disciples go and teach all nations, baptizing them ; but never said, if they be sick and weak, do not baptize them." At last Caleb prevails, and secures the promise of baptism on the next day, if the weather allows. "The night continued tempestuous, and he called often betwixt his slumbers to know what weather?" But the day was sunny and calm, and in the afternoon the whole company proceeded in three coaches, with some on foot, to the house by the river which had been prepared. Caleb would not lie on the pillows arranged on the knees of his father and mother, but insisted on sitting up. He is kept by the fire in the house whilst his father speaks from most suitably chosen words—they *did* know their Bibles in Bunyan's day—" And when he would not be persuaded, we ceased, saying: The will of the Lord be done ". The fulness of experiential meaning, the positive note of the divine gift in baptism, comes out in the father's exhortation, who " desired now to witness to it as the will of God, showing the Commands for it, Signification of it, and ends that should be proposed in it, desiring they might be in them, and that Presence which might make it to both his Sons the Communion of the Death and Resurrection of Christ to such a putting him on (in virtue of all his Offices), as might manifest their being as it were—thenceforth new-died [dyed] with, or tinged into Christ, to their favour of him in all things, in newness of Nature and life ". The two boys, Caleb and his brother, were then baptized, and Caleb was received by his father into a warm blanket, saying as soon as he could speak, " I am very well, father ", as he had said to the doubtful administrator, " I am not afraid ". On his way home in the coach he told his mother and father: " He had very great joy in Communion with God coming up out of the Water, when he could not express it, his breath failing through some water that went into his mouth (which he merrily said, he had forgot to shut) ". The next day but one a meeting of the Church was held in his room, that he might have the privilege of the Lord's Supper with them, " wherein to the eye of Faith Christ would be evidently set forth, crucified before him, for his consolation ".

Naturally enough, the mother is not so prominent in this record as the father, who is both physician and minister as well. But she moves in and out of the sick-room, and sits with her boy in fullest communion. " Mother," he says to her once, " I love your company dearly." It is the mother who, like another mother, treasures these things in her heart, and writes them down secretly, so that we have some of the material for this record through her. " God loves me, mother, and sometimes I love the Lord." Does not that bear the hallmark of truth upon it? It is pleasant to hear of the service rendered by Abraham Cheare, the Baptist verse-maker, who was a friend of the family. Caleb is fond of repeating his verses. After some of them his mother says: "And do you remember, Child, what he saith of young Isaacs?" "Yea, Mother," said he; and then further repeated some of these concerning youth:

> Young Isaacs who lift up their eyes,
>   And meditate in fields;
> Young Jacobs who the Blessing prize,
>   This age but seldom yields.
> Few Samuels leaving youthful playes,
>   To Temple-work resign'd;
> Few do as these, in youthful dayes
>   Their great Creator mind.
> How precious Obadiahs be
>   That fearèd God in youth:
> How seldom Timothys we see,
>   Vers'd in the Word of Truth. . . .
> Few tender-hearted Youths as was
>   Josiah, Judah's king;
> Hosannah in the high'st, alas,
>   How seldom children sing!

It is worthy of note that even in those stern old days they were making the same complaints about the degeneracy of youth as we hear to-day and as our great-grandchildren will hear in their turn. And they *were* stern old days. There is something rather grim in the attitude of the father to the son, something Spartan and Stoic at least, as when the child says that his bones are sore, and the father replies, "Ay, Child, but your soul is not"; or when Caleb asks, "Do not you think that death is troublesome?" and the old Cromwellian replies, "Yes, Child, a little to the flesh." Yet there is deep feeling beneath this religious Stoicism. The boy can thank God for tender parents on earth as in heaven. Even if there is respectful timidity when the sick boy says to his father, writing in the room, "Father, will it not disturb you to talk with me?" there is surely the heart's knowledge of affection sure and deep when the sufferer looks up from his bed of affliction and says: "Father, you be my dear father." That. I think, is significant of the whole book. We turn away from the stilted language of the "anagrams" and "acrosticks" with which the older and younger friends of Caleb Vernon adorn his hearse; they leave us cold, if not repelled; most people to-day would turn away also from the unnaturalness of the experience of a Bunyan, as it seems, on the lips of a boy of twelve. We have more patience to-day with literary precocities than with religious, though as we judge we shall be judged by a later generation. But underneath these forms alien to our expression there is the common human nature and the sincerity of a religious experience akin to ours. The strength of such a home was in its religion, and its religion did inspire and sustain a loyalty to the home ties and the home duties which is the true consecration of such human relationships.

(2) A BAPTIST SOLDIER (WILLIAM ALLEN)

One of many services rendered by Dr. Whitley's *A History of British Baptists* is to have brought out the great place taken by Baptists in Cromwell's " New Model Army ". A typical figure amongst them, about which we are exceedingly well informed, is that of William Allen,[1] whose name appears more than once in Carlyle's *Letters and Speeches of Oliver Cromwell*. To Carlyle, Adjutant-General Allen was " a most authentic earnest man ... a strenuous Anabaptist ... a rugged, true-hearted, not easily governable man ; given to Fifth-Monarchy and other notions, though with a strong head to control them ". This impression is confirmed when we identify him with the Trooper Allen (as Carlyle wrongly refused to do) who brought the letter of the soldiers to Major-General Skippon in 1647.[2] Allen stated then, in his examination, that he was a Warwickshire man who had been a feltmaker by trade in Southwark. He had served in Essex's army under Colonel Holles, till he was taken prisoner at Brentford. After seven days of captivity, he was condemned with seventeen others to be hanged ; then every tenth man was drawn out to be hanged ; finally he was dismissed with the others. He was wounded at the first battle of Newbury and again at Henley, when Skippon rewarded him with five shillings. If only Allen had written for us a few " letters from the front " the historian would have been more grateful to him than for what he did write—with the one exception of the account of the famous " Windsor Prayer Meeting ". Carlyle's pages have made us familiar with that gathering of army leaders meeting for three days of prayer in the *impasse* to

[1] Uncle of the Caleb Vernon who was the subject of the preceding study.
[2] See *The Clarke Papers*, ed. Firth, i, p. 432 and A. S. P. Woodhouse, *Puritanism and Liberty: Debates from the Clarke MSS. with Supplementary Documents*, 1938.

which an impracticable Parliament and a shifty king have brought them, retracing their steps to the point at which they had exchanged straightforward action for political scheming, and led at last to the historic conclusion " that it was our duty, if ever the Lord brought us back again in peace, to call Charles Stuart, that man of blood, to an account for that blood he had shed and mischief he had done to his utmost, against the Lord's Cause and People in these poor Nations ".

Military movements brought William Allen and John Vernon into Devonshire, where they married sisters of the name of Huish, their father being James Huish, of Sidbury. The names of Allen and Vernon stand on the church-roll of Dalwood, in Dorset, and often recur together in later records and books, as in the prefaces they both contribute to the religious autobiography of Deborah Huish, their sister-in-law (which is entitled *The Captive taken from the Strong*, and was written down from her lips by William Allen). But this was in later days of sorrowful leisure, after Allen had been so disappointed in his leader. His first disillusionment with Cromwell appears in an intercepted letter of his of 1654,[1] written soon after the Protectorate began, in which he says: " As to the person in chief place, I confess I love and honour him, for the honour God hath put upon him, and I trust will yet continue ; I mean that of uprightheartedness to the Lord, though this last change . . . hath more stumbled me than ever any did ; and I have still many thoughts of heart concerning it." He was, in fact, coming to think of the Lord Protector as Labour has often thought of its official leaders—who need watching, to say the least. Yet at the same time he will not resign his commission, and argues against a friend who has done so, on the ground that he can exercise more effective influence where he is: " I trust I shall not, upon the account of honourable or other worldly respects, stay a day longer in employment than I judge I may do more good in than out." Allen was then in Dublin[2] whither he had gone as " Adjutant-General of the Horse " in 1651, and he also appears as a com-

---

[1] Thurloe, *Collection of State Papers*, ii, p. 214 (App. 6).

[2] Allen's services in Ireland were very great, as may be seen in Dunlop's *Ireland under the Commonwealth*. He was also one of the thinkers and organizers who suggested grouping all the Baptist Churches into associations ; the military led to the ecclesiastical organization (Whitley, p. 90).

missioner for the settlement of Ulster. But it was not long before his dissatisfaction with Cromwell led to an open collision. They had an interview in London which, according to Allen, made the Protector very angry, though Allen complains that he was not allowed to say as much as he wanted to, since the Protector did most of the talking. Allen came down to Devonshire, where his movements and talk aroused suspicion that he was plotting. Finally he was dramatically arrested when in bed at his father-in-law's house by several soldiers armed with sword and pistol. Allen writes in defence of himself and in protest against such treatment after thirteen years of faithful service. His defence was hardly likely to smooth the ruffled plumage of his old commander, for he says, in the course of a letter[1] to Oliver:—

> You are also pleased to tax me with having as light an esteem of you as of C. S. [Charles Stuart], though neither did any word in my letter nor any action of mine ever give you ground for such a surmise. What my esteem hath been of you in some verticall forsaking [sic] days I believe you can remember ; and I can truly say, if I have erred, it hath been, I fear, in esteeming too highly of you. The different esteem I yet have of your Lordship from the other part is this ; I could freely engage against the other as formerly, but I durst not lift a hand against you, nor join with or advise the doing of it.

Cromwell's own view of the situation is given in the letter to his Exeter agent: "Adjutant-General Allen doth very ill offices by multiplying dissatisfaction in the minds of men to the present Government." Nevertheless Allen was permitted to return to his post in Ireland, though difficulties were not ended. How could they be for two such men? In 1657 we hear of Allen's resignation to Henry Cromwell, who records the impression Allen made on him[2]:—

> Subtile and grave Mr. Allen brought up the rear and was more ingenuous than the rest in declaring that the ground of his dissatisfaction took its rise from the first change of the government, foreseeing that they should be no way able to answer the end for which they were first engaged ; and being now more fully convinced of it, and looking upon himself as formerly discharged by his highness, he thought it best for him to draw to a more retired position.

[1] Thurloe, *op. cit.*, iii, p. 140.
[2] Thurloe, *op. cit.*, v, pp. 670-2.

We hear of Allen and Vernon again in Devonshire just after the death of the Protector. Sir John Coplestone has his eye upon them,[1] as the late Protector had commanded, for they are men who must be watched: "Certainly they are persons of as much venom and revenge as any whatever and will not spare to adventure on anything that may give them the least hope of success." Allen's displacements from military service, like the repeated banishments of Athanasius, reflected the vicissitudes of the time, for he was made a colonel of horse by the restored Long Parliament in 1659, only to be removed by Monck in 1660. Soon after this he was imprisoned for "endeavouring to debauch some of the soldiers from their obedience, and likewise suspected of being dangerous to the State". In the following year he and John Vernon were sent into exile, and the last we hear of Allen is an elegy over his brother-in-law's death in 1666.[2] Some of its lines surely express the writer's own disappointment with the times:—

> His soul did mourn in secret for such pride
> He found with many long before he died:
> To see a worldly, formal, selfish spirit
> 'Mongst men professing Heaven to inherit.

But the fullest account of his attitude is to be found in his *Word to the Army,* a pamphlet of twenty pages issued in 1660. In this, as in his *Faithful Memorial* of the preceding year (which gives the account of the Windsor Prayer Meeting), he reviews the decline of the true cause, and speaks of Cromwell in his virtual kingship as "a ghost from the grave" of the Stuarts. The army has been guilty of "King-craft and worse than Bishop-like trapannings". He sees a grim meaning in the taking away of the Protector on the very anniversary of his victories at Dunbar and Worcester. The only true way to a Magna Charta is to acknowledge God.

We may sympathize with this Baptist condemnation of Oliver as a "worldly politician" (the phrase is S. R. Gardiner's) without for one minute thinking that Allen could have succeeded where Oliver had failed, even though he had been Oliver. There are situations in which events demonstrate

[1] *Ibid. op. cit.,* vii, p. 385.
[2] *Bochim* (British Museum, Lutt. I, 153).

their power over men,[1] and the situation becomes too big for them, as recent events have taught us. There is no short cut to a kingdom of the saints, as the Fifth-Monarchy men thought, and the Parliament supposed to be made up of saints was at least as ineffective as any other. But through human failure, as well as human success, we can recognize and admire the presence of great aims, pursued with conscience and with courage. William Allen and his comrades can claim an interest of eternity as well as of time. As S. R. Gardiner remarks: "It was because the spear of Parliamentarism was tipped with Puritanism that the strife appeals to all who are attracted by the spectacle of unselfish human emotion resolving itself into action".[2] The militant Puritanism of that age was largely Baptist.

(3) A Baptist Reformer (Thomas Lambe)

If Carlyle had come across a little four-page tract, the only known copy of which seems to be that in the Angus Library,[3] he might have treated it in the same manner as *The Chronicle of Jocelin of Brakelond*, and made it the basis of a miniature *Past and Present*. The title of the tract is, *An Appeal to the Parliament concerning the Poor, that there may not be a Beggar in England*. It is signed "T. L.", the initials of Thomas Lambe, a well-known Baptist of the seventeenth century, who has found his way into the *Dictionary of National Biography*, though at the cost of some confusion with another Baptist of the same name. It bears the arresting date of 1660, the year of the great "Settlement", upon which Carlyle pours such scorn in the book I have named. That date gives significance to the opening words of the tract: "In the midst of many and great Undertakings, let not a Settlement for the *Poor* be forgotten." The surprising thing about this tract is its modernity. Here we have proposals for Labour Exchanges, Parish Councils (of a sort), and the drafting of unemployed labour to industrial centres. Even the pressure on the middle classes, which we think peculiarly our own

---

[1] Cf. Lord Grey, *Twenty-five Years*, p. 51: "There is in great affairs so much more, as a rule, in the minds of the events (if such an expression may be used) than in the minds of the chief actors."
[2] *Cromwell's Place in History*, p. 22.
[3] Reprinted in the *Baptist Quarterly*, i, 3, pp. 128-31.

difficulty, is in view, for the writer compares them with "small Iron Creepers in a chimney" (the iron "dogs" which supported the burning wood on the hearth) "who bear the burden and heat of the Fire, until they be wasted to Sinders".

Thomas Lambe believes with Carlyle that everything depends on the men you put in office, and he believes also that the problems of poverty and unemployment must be faced locally. Each parish is to "agree with some Able Man, or Men, that rightly understandeth their Work". These representatives of the parish will divide their problem into three parts. They will assist the old, the impotent, and young children by a parish levy; they will help those whose work does not bring in a living wage; they will group the unemployed in tens or twenties and arrange either for them to be supplied with work from some employer, or for them to be drafted to centres in which there is need of hands. The social problem is envisaged as the disproportionate distribution of potential workers and the need for a proper distribution of them. But it is also recognized that "though there may be work enough, yet the Idle will not come for it", so that authority will be necessary. In some parishes a decayed industry must be replaced by something new. In others, where there is no poverty (instances near London are given), contributions must be raised for more necessitous districts.

The Labour Exchange proposed is to be a centre trough which would-be employers and the unemployed can be brought into contact, where boys can find masters to whom they may be apprenticed, where girls may find apprenticeship or service. But in regard to such service for girls, Thomas Lambe is singularly up to date in his fear of "blind alleys"; the girls are not to go to service "until they be first Taught to Spin, Knit, Sew, learn some Trade, or way of livelihood; who else are neither fit for Service, nor can in aftertimes do any thing for themselves". Further, there is to be ready access to Justices of the Peace for complaints of neglect or oppression, and the judges of assizes and sessions are to enforce justice in this matter and to publish the law in regard to it. The wants of the poor must be supplied before legal measures are to be taken against them. Part of Lambe's scheme is a census of city populations. He urges that all this is everybody's business and not simply the concern of Parliament men. "If any Object the Trouble: To have such Multitudes of Beggars in this fruitful Kingdom, is not that trouble? To hear them cry and not give, is not that trouble? To hear their cry and give, is trouble also; not knowing whether it doth good or harm."

The little tract is a good example of that "social conscience" which is by no means such a discovery of yesterday as is sometimes thought. It illustrates the sense of serious moral responsibility,[1] as well as the social sympathies which are certainly promoted by Baptist principles.

(4) A Baptist Teacher (Benjamin Keach)

On a certain autumn Thursday in the year 1664, between the hours of eleven and one, groups of people stood in the market-place of Winslow (in Bucks) curiously or sympathetically watching the pillory and a young man who had his head and his hands fixed in it. Over his head, as over his Lord's so long before, was an inscription which the more learned spelt out to their neighbours: "For writing, printing and publishing a schismatical Book, intitled, *The Child's Instructor, or a New and Easy Primmer.*" Some of them had seen his face turned and his hands outstretched to them before, in the less constraining attitude of the pulpit, for he was a preacher; others were perhaps wearing clothes at which he had stitched, for he was a tailor. Presently there was a little stir as the hangman came forward and kindled a small bonfire in front of the captive. When it was burning sufficiently, he thrust into it a very little book—the book to which the inscription referred. No copy of that edition has come down to us, but Benjamin Keach lived to re-write and re-publish it, just as Jeremiah, through Baruch, re-wrote and re-published his own burnt prophecies. A characteristic little frontispiece in the earliest surviving edition (that of about a quarter of a century later) depicts two godly youths on the narrow way, one praying and one advancing, whilst a vener-

---

[1] Cf. the remark made in a letter by Thomas Arnold of Rugby: "When I look round upon boys or men, there seems to me some one point or quality, which distinguishes really noble persons from ordinary ones; it is not religious feeling—it is not honesty or kindness; but it seems to be moral thoughtfulness" (Stanley's *Life of Arnold*, end of chap. viii).

able friend, comfortably seated, holds out the open page of Scripture. Below is the alternative, where a horned and clawed devil lurks in a pit at the end of the broad way; inset are two episodes of the journey, in one of which the foolish youth has his mincing steps escorted by two gaily bedizened damsels, whilst in the other, three players are gathered around the card-table. They did not leave much to the imagination in those seventeenth-century days.

The book is of considerable interest to the educationist, and amply deserves the commendatory preface by Hanserd Knollys. We begin with the alphabet and a short series of spelling lessons. Then follow "Precepts for Children" in verse, which mingle with the Christian appeal adjurations to spell rightly; that mixture, with a preponderance of the appeal, is characteristic of the whole book. After a few Scripture sentences broken up into syllables, we come to the first of a series of three catechisms, suited respectively to the ages of "between three and four", "ten", and "mature age"—quite on the principle of the "graded school" of our days! These are of interest as giving cross-sections of the presumptive religious capabilities at these several ages. The child of three or four learns that Methuselah was the oldest man that ever lived, that God is a Spirit, and that salvation is by conversion; the moral lessons he needs are put into verse, evidently to be memorized. He is zealously warned against giving his mind to play. Next comes his brother of ten, who is plunged into deeper waters of theological inquiry. Keach must have felt this, for when the father asks "Who is God?" the child is at least taught candour in his reply: "I do not know very well; is he not an old man?", the reason being that "God made Man in his own Image". But the child's chief difficulty, as his instructor conceives him, is in the serious temptation to defer religious decision to a later age. "Father," he says plaintively, "I am very young" (ten!), "may I not do as other Children do, and defer the minding of these things, until I am older?" But the father promptly ascribes such thoughts to the inspiration of the devil, and grimly counters with the words, "Do you not see many *little* Graves as well as great ones?", and recounts the experience of precocious infants and young children, including a girl of nine, who rises to the ripe experience of a Bunyan, and after long waiting for an answer to prayer says, "Well, I venture my

Soul upon Christ." Here the father does not mince matters.
" Are you," he says to this pathetic child of ten, " old enough
to be damn'd and too young to be sav'd? " No wonder that
the child's last word is, " My dear Father, I can hold out no
longer, my Heart is smitten, and my Soul trembles", and
forthwith chants the ten commandments in a versified form.
There is now a digression, in which the father addresses his
daughters and warns them against the worldly life of the
Restoration, with its " rowling Eyes and amorous Glances ".
Again there is a plaintive interjection, for one daughter says,
" Doth not God allow some Things for Ornaments? ", and
the father is honest enough to remember Rebekah. For the
versified duties of the daughters Benjamin Keach feels that
he cannot do better than borrow from Abraham Cheare, the
contemporary Baptist verse-maker, whose verses were sung
by little Caleb Vernon also:

> When by Spectators I am told
> What Beauty doth adorn me,
> Or in a glass when I behold
> How sweetly God did form me:
> Hath God such comeliness display'd
> And on me made to dwell,
> What pitty such a pretty Maid
> As I should go to Hell.

The Youth's Catechism which follows is a whole body of
divinity, too long for notice and for most men to-day too
tedious, followed by an exposition of the Lord's Prayer. The
subject of Believers' Baptism is well handled, without bitter-
ness against " our Godly Brethren, who differ from us".
The " Advice to Youth ", in verse, gives an interesting
glimpse of the pious youth and his beginning of the day. He
thanks God for preservation during the night, and prays for
grace during the day. He goes downstairs, salutes the other
members of the family, and proceeds to wash his hands (at the
pump) and comb his head, paying due attention to the cleanli-
ness of his clothes. After the reading of Scripture and prayer,
he is ready either to sit at table or to wait on his parents. He
is particularly careful neither to talk nor to stare in the faces
of his parents. The rest of the book is mainly concerned with
worldly information, " Thirty days hath September ", the

writing of a receipt, punctuation, weights and measures, and a dictionary of hard words. But we return to the theme of the frontispiece at the end, where both the Devil and Christ solicit an ungodly youth. Then Christ passes from the scene, and is replaced by a doctor, whose only prescription for aching head and cold feet is " Call upon God for you will die ", and the Doctor is duly followed by Death. They made it all very plain in those days of our forefathers.

Keach eventually became a leading figure amongst London Baptists, and, as we shall see, the pioneer of congregational hymn-singing. He returned to the theme of " War with the Devil ", or the Young Man's Conflict with the Powers of Darkness, in 1673. In this use of religious allegory he was, as Dr. Whitley has pointed out,[1] a precursor of Bunyan. But Keach's narrative, though reaching twenty-two editions within a century, lacks that insight into the realities of human life which has given Bunyan his place amongst the immortals.

(5) A BAPTIST CHURCH
(THAMES STREET, NEWGATE STREET, CRIPPLEGATE)

Some aspects of Baptist personality in the seventeenth and eighteenth centuries are best revealed by the study of a Baptist Church of those days. Here we shall see the social interaction of Baptists within the little world of religious fellowship which they created for themselves, the disputes which agitated them, the methods of their corporate life as expressing their convictions, the human passions that beset the Christian minister. All these aspects are illustrated in a Church-Book of the Baptist Church gathered by the well-known Hanserd Knollys about 1642, though its continuous record does not begin till a year or two before his death in 1691.[2] The manuscript, in many different hands which belongs to the Angus Library of Regent's Park College, is found in a vellum-covered volume, with clasps, its size being 16 in. by 6 in. The book is not the Minute-Book of the Church (to which reference is occasionally made), though for part of the period

---

[1] *A History of British Baptists*, pp. 132, 133.
[2] Before it reached Thames Street, it had met in Colman Street, Wapping (Tower Street), Artichoke Lane, Booby Lane. It never owned a building and is now extinct (Whitley).

covered it seems to have been used as a Minute-Book ; originally, the record might better be called a Discipline Book, in which the more private and personal matters were recorded. The earliest date is September 26, 1689, and the latest Christmas Day, 1723. Four regular pastorates are included, though we have only the first year of the fourth, viz. those of Robert Steed, who became co-pastor with Knollys in 1689, and died whilst still in office in 1700; David Crosley, who was ordained in January 1702-3 and expelled on August 14, 1709 ; John Skepp, ordained September 7, 1714, died in office, December 1, 1721 ; Humphrey Barrow, ordained June 5, 1723, died in office, 1727. The Church had 113 members in 1689 and 212 in 1721. It was one of some twenty-six Baptist Churches of all types to be found at this time in London, Southwark, and Westminster, which together had a population of over half a million.[1] Probably its inner life and problems may be taken as fairly typical of a " gathered " community at the time, of what we now call the Congregational polity.

(a) *The Discipline Book*

The first point to be made is that the study of such a record is the best way to realize with accuracy and proper emphasis what the principles of a denomination really mean. Instead of conventional and colourless statements, which admit of very different applications, we have here a picture of real life, with men and women acting under the stress of living convictions. In the meeting-place, first in George Yard, Thames Street (1688), some years later at the Bagnio, Newgate Street, and a little later still at Curriers' Hall, Cripplegate, we listen to the speech of a solemn and intensely earnest group of men and women, and we find where their interest really lay. It was not the fact, as is often supposed, that their chief concern was the negative one of " independency ", i.e. of repudiating any interference from without ; their concern was the positive one of maintaining what they held to be the Christian standard of faith and conduct within. We may feel that their microscopic examination of the lives and thoughts of their fellow-members was not wholly healthy, and had grave perils ;

---

[1] Whitley, *History*, p. 181.

yet even when we criticize their methods, we must admit that the endeavour to maintain a high quality of Christian life was itself a noble one, and the logical and necessary outcome of their principles. They were a separated Church of men and women; they were bound to insist on a Christian ethic, the expression of a Christian faith which should stand out emphatically from the conventionalism and loose morals of the age.

For convenience, we may confine ourselves under this head to the Discipline Book kept by Robert Steed from 1689 to 1700.[1] There seem to have been only about a score of cases of discipline in the course of the dozen years, which is a remarkable testimony to character, when we consider the rigorous scrutiny and the social level from which most, perhaps all, of the membership was drawn. The occupation of some is characterized in the list of members: —

> A Taylor in Hungerford Market.
> A chambermaid to Squ. Barrington.
> The daughter of her that keeps the meeting-house.
> A schoolmaster in Gravell Lane.

Half a dozen of the cases of discipline illustrate the Scriptural truth that the love of money is a root of all kinds of evil. Two women members were convicted of having obtained money under false pretences from another woman—her little all of £40 saved up for old age. They told her that her capital would be increased if she lent it, but, in fact, the money was needed by one of these delinquents to pay her debts. They were both excluded from membership. Brother Brooksby, as a result of a transaction in hops with a member of another church, called him a rascal and a knave, and brought a law-suit against him. The matter received careful attention, but Brother Brooksby overreached himself by putting in a document that was proved to be a forgery; exit Brother Brooksby. Brother Leeson not only failed to meet what was due to his father-in-law, but aggravated this by behaving "as a rude Hector", as witnessed by a letter of threats duly read to the Church. Brother Hind also failed to pay his debts, but the trouble here was intemperance in drink.

---

[1] Published in the *Baptist Quarterly*, July and October, 1922.

Sister Foster was found guilty of a breach of trust in regard to some goods deposited in her keeping and was proved a liar. In two cases the trouble was between husband and wife. A journeyman shoemaker was excluded for wife-beating and for failing through idleness to make proper provision for his family. In another instance the husband complained of the wife's bad language to him. After due examination, it was decided "that deep distressing poverty had afflicted her through his incapacity or negligence to get a livelihood or subsistence, whereby great provocations had been given her to speak and act unadvisedly"; the case was admonition and temporary suspension. Another set of domestic problems meets us in the relations of master and apprentice. Brother Hake, an apprentice to Brother Dennis, a scrivener, was charged with negligence and disobedience and with calumniating his master and mistress to their neighbours. Young Hake was brought up before the Church to express his repentance, but threw out a hint that he was not content with the food he got, and was eventually again brought up by his master. This time he had thrown down and beaten another apprentice and threatened this youth's master when he came to his rescue. When found about the place next morning and told to be gone, " he held up his fists against Mr. Reep, and told him it was well it was Sunday morning, otherwise had it been another day he would have beaten Mr. Reep". This young swashbuckler's fault was aggravated because Mr. Reep had been friendly with him. It was testified that Hake "had idly spent his time at Coffee houses playing at draffts. And that one time Mr. Reep aforesaid playing with him and having won the game of him, He making him pay the forfeit which was a dish of Coffee, He fell out with Mr. Reep and sayd as soon as he was gone that he had about him that which would do Mr. Reep's business which he could find in his heart to make use off; which was a penknife he had in his pocket to stab him withall". It was unfortunate for young Hake that he was born before the time of the Boy Scouts; they might have made an excellent fellow of him. But the stern Church sent him into the outer darkness, to flourish that scrivener's penknife of his beyond our ken. Another apprentice in trouble was called Joseph Faircloth, a haberdasher, who did not live up to his first name if he did to his second, for he became too intimate with a cheesemonger's wife, who kept him out late. These London 'prentices must have given their masters a world of trouble. (Another apprentice case of the same kind is reported.) There are two instances in which action is taken for non-attendance at meetings; the defence was the experience of spiritual temptations, which should have been regarded as a reason for attending, not for stopping away; in two others there were frustrated attempts to get back on the Church roll without due warrant. The only instance of excommunication for heresy—that of a man and his wife who denied the divine nature of Christ—was quite fairly dealt with. The only other type of case left unnoticed is that of a man who persisted in preaching elsewhere at the public meetings, then called "Lectures", without seeming to the Church to have competent gifts for it. The way in which the Church dealt with him is both drastic and ingenious, though I do not suggest that *they* saw the subtle humour of it. They condemned him for preaching without formal approval by the Church, for neglect of his business whilst he went preaching, with the result that he had to compound with his creditors, and also for failing to be in his place in the Church to which he belonged whilst he was away preaching elsewhere! His exclusion, after admonition, only served to harden him in his evil courses, for we read that "instead of repenting he turned from the truth and, joyned with them that sprinkl infants, is ordained the pastor of a pbiterian [i.e. Presbyterian] congregation at Epping in Essex ".

These details are of interest in themselves, and help us to reconstruct a living picture of the life and relations of a Separatist Church of the congregational order at the close of the seventeenth century. But the purpose for which they are here mentioned is to show how seriously these people took what is, after all, the foundation principle of a separated or gathered Church—the character and conduct of its membership. Whatever we may think about the perils or the impossibility of exercising any such discipline to-day, at least we ought to realize that the discipline was an honest attempt to carry out the principles theoretically expressed in the self-governing polity. As long as that polity is retained, it would seem that both Baptists and Congregationalists are committed to the principle underlying it, and this Discipline Book shows us what that principle really means when taken as seriously as it was in Newgate Street.

The best example, however, of the thoroughness with which questions of discipline were handled is contained in a record of the Church Book subsequent to that Discipline Book of which I have been speaking. The particular example is a painful one, and some of its details could not well be made public. It is the story of the downfall of David Crosley, of which this is the only full record. He and his cousin, William Mitchell, had done a great evangelistic work in Yorkshire and Lancashire, and the Baptist Churches that ultimately sprang from their joint labours were many. He came into prominence in the south through a sermon preached at a Presbyterian church when he was twenty-two. He had been staying in the house of John Strudwick (where Bunyan had died three years before), and opposite him as he sat at the dinner-table was a tapestry depicting Samson in combat with the lion he slew. This seized his imagination, and led to the sermon called "Samson a type of Christ", in the manner of the allegorical preaching of the time. A bookseller who heard it there and then proposed to print it, and a thousand copies were sold in six months. After the death of Robert Steed in 1700 he was invited to succeed him, and was ordained at the Bagnio in January 1702-3, being then about thirty-three. His ministry was eminently successful, as we might have expected from his record; but from about 1707 rumours were in circulation that the popular minister was drinking too freely, even for that tolerant age, and that his behaviour towards women gave rise to grave suspicions. For a long time the rumours were discredited by most, who felt, as is said, that "he could not if guilty be so helped in his ministry". It is the story of Hawthorne's *Scarlet Letter* over again, though on a lower and coarser level. At length the Church was bound to deal with it.

I have been greatly impressed by the thorough and just manner in which the leaders of the Church dealt with this painful scandal. The affidavits of the witnesses are given in full; their evidence was carefully tested, and full opportunity was given to David Crosley to defend himself. He acknowledged drunkenness, and was convicted of lying in the course of the very deliberate proceedings, but he maintained to the end his innocence in the gravest features of the case. There can be little doubt, however, in the mind of anyone who reads the documents and follows the course of events, that

David Crosley was guilty of immoral conduct, and that the Church was fully justified in its ultimate act of excommunication, in which there was full unanimity. After prayer, there was a careful statement of the charges proved by " the Brother that was the mouth of the Church ", with references to the Scriptures that bore on each point. The brother then proceeded: —

You, the Church of Jesus Christ, having judged him guilty of these gross sins, and having also judged it not for the glory of God, nor for the honour of this Church that such a one should be continued in the communion of this Church (and after silence, the Brother appointed expressed the sentence in these words):—

Therefore, we do in the name of our Lord Jesus, and in the name and authority of this Church, withdraw from our Brother David Crosley, for his disorderly walking, and we put him out of union, and Communion, of this Church, until the Lord give him repentance to the satisfaction of the Church.

The Church at Tottlebank, Lancashire, of which Crosley had been minister for nine years before coming to London, refused to believe him guilty, but they never had the evidence before them. If we needed confirmation, it would lie in the fact that similar charges were brought against him in the north again in 1719, and he was virtually excommunicated in the following year. Yet his powers as a preacher remained, and at the age of seventy-two he could hold an open-air audience of four thousand people. He died in 1744, bequeathing us one of those perplexing problems of human inconsistency—or human frailty. As I turn over these manuscript pages of his story, I seem to see a man temperamentally weak by the very qualities that made him effective as a popular preacher, poised in unstable moral equilibrium, and the more able to understand the struggles of other men—till the habituation of evil thought made evil act easy, and the finer edge of moral judgment was blunted. As an older man, when the passions of youth were left behind, he seems to have won and kept the respect of others, and George Whitefield writes a preface to the republication of his famous sermon on " Samson a type of Christ ". Strudwick's tapestry was a prophetic foreshadowing of his own life, for David Crosley was something of a Samson in his strength and in his weakness.

(b) *The Controversy about Hymn-singing*

The past is strewn with the ashes of controversies where the fires of passion once burnt fiercely, and at least one interesting example of this is afforded by the book before us. At the beginning of 1693 a group of twenty-two malcontents from the Church of Horsley Down, Southwark, under the ministry of Benjamin Keach, sought fellowship with the Bagnio Church under Robert Steed, "being dissatisfied with their setting up of common set form singing after it had been exploded by the Baptized Churches as a humane invention; and also being grieved with the manner of their proceeding with them when they declared their dissatisfaction with their introducing that innovation". Thereon hangs a tale of some length. The honour of first introducing hymns into the regular worship of an English congregation, established or dissenting, belongs to Benjamin Keach,[1] and his book of three hundred hymns, called *Spiritual Melody*, and published in 1691, was the first hymn-book to be so used, though he had published hymns for children to learn as early as 1664. None of his hymns has survived in common use, and had the leaders of this "split" from his Church argued that Keach's hymns were doggerel, instead of arguing against the general principle of hymn-singing, we might have sympathized with them. Here are some specimens:—

> Our wounds do stink and are corrupt,
>   Hard swellings we do see;
> We want a little ointment, Lord,
>   Let us more humble be.   (p. 173.)

> Repentance like a bucket is
>   To pump the water out;
> For leaky is our ship, alas,
>   Which makes us look about.   (p. 254.)

> Here meets them now that worm that gnaws,
>   And plucks their bowels out;
> The pit, too, on them shuts her jaws,
>   This dreadful is, no doubt.   (p. 312.)

[1] Cf. Whitley, *op. cit.*, pp. 187, 188.

However, it was not the quality of the hymns, but the principle of hymn-singing (as distinct from singing Scriptural psalms) that was at issue. Benjamin Keach's practice of hymn-singing, first introduced at the Communion Service, was spreading amongst Particular Baptist Churches, though vigorously attacked. In the same year as Keach published the first hymn-book, he issued an *apologia* for his practice, entitled *The Breach Repaired in God's Worship*, in which he elevates the practice to a *Sacred Truth of the Gospel* (p. vi), and couples its neglect with that of the ministry as the two chief causes of " our sad witherings ". A favourite proof-text of his was Exod. xxxii. 18, " the noise of them that sing do I hear ", and he argues quite reasonably that " one man's voice could not have made such a noise ", therefore the singing must have been congregational ; nor is he deterred by the fact which his opponents gleefully pointed out, that this congregation was singing to the praise of the Golden Calf. One of these opponents was Robert Steed, which explains why the group of malcontents with Keach sought refuge at the Bagnio Church. In 1691 Steed published *An Epistle . . . concerning Singing*, denouncing the practice on the following grounds. Singing by a set stinted form is an invention of man, being of the same quality as, if not worse than, common stinted set-form prayers, or even infant sprinkling. It is artificial, and therefore alien to the free motions of the Spirit of God. We should have the true and spontaneous song if we had more of the Holy Spirit. As for arguments drawn from the music of the Old Testament, all *that* is done away in Christ. Moreover, some cannot sing, not having tunable voices, and women ought anyhow to keep silence in the churches. I think we must admire Robert Steed's ingenuity, whilst we differ from his conclusions. But the most important point to notice in this ancient and long-settled controversy is that both sides seem to us wrong-headed in their arguments. To us, hymn-singing is neither a Gospel ordinance to be neglected at our soul's peril, nor a wicked innovation, displaying the policy of Satan ; it is of practical use in worship, and that settles the matter. We have moved away from the ground of Scriptural authority in such matters to the modern ground of the evidence of religious experience. It is these great changes, often unrecognized, that do settle most of the controversies, not the particular arguments employed. The dispute about hymn-singing and many another bone of contention lies forgotten; but it is worth while to hunt it out from the dark corner where it lies to remind us that some of our own issues may suffer the same fate, and be settled, not by our arguments, but by the inevitable course of things and their intrinsic worth. This does not mean any lack of respect for the seriousness displayed in the endeavour to refer details of practice to evangelical principles.

(6) A BAPTIST WRITER (ANN DUTTON)

The Baptist passion for liberty which characterized the seventeenth century and the Baptist awakening to the need for missionary work shortly before the nineteenth century are like two great waves, which have between them the trough of the hyper-Calvinism and the spiritual lethargy of Baptist life in the eighteenth century. It is only fair to show the general character of this period, as it is reflected in a particular life, in order to bring out the perils and weaknesses of this type of religious experience, whether Baptist or not. We take as our example a copious writer, whose monument once recorded "twenty-five volumes of choice Letters to friends and thirty-eight Tracts on Divine and Spiritual Subjects",[1] though they are doubtless entirely unknown to the present reader. Her revealing account of herself is interesting as a "human document", but the study of it will also test our power of sympathy, for underneath all the vanities and frailties that are so apparent within the narrow theological frame, there is still a genuine passion for God; in her own phrase, she was "an ascending Spark in Christ's vehement flame".

If Ann had been born a couple of centuries later she would doubtless have become a leading lady on the denominational platform. If Ann had been born in the Court circles of her own day she might have become another Countess of Yarmouth, by her good looks, her lively imagination, and her sensuous disposition. As it was, "she aspired to be the

[1] J. C. Whitebrook in *Transactions of the Baptist Historical Society*, vol. vii, Nos. 3 and 4, pp. 129 ff. He devotes himself chiefly to her controversies and correspondence with Wesley, Whitefield, Cudworth and others. The present study is confined to the volume of autobiography.

Countess of Huntingdon of the denomination".[1] Her portrait suggests a Court beauty rather than a Baptist minister's wife—though, indeed, she was never quite that, for Mr. Dutton would always be "Mrs. Dutton's husband". Here is an accurate description of the portrait as given by a caustic biographer: "It represents her tossing a very shapely little head, on which her own hair is tired high, to fall in large curly ringlets on either side of a smooth, well-poised neck. A silk gown, tight in sleeves and waist, is rucked in rolled chiffon, décolleté, with gathered sleeves ribboned at the insertion. Her expression is what our ancestors would have called 'sprightly', and quite explains much of the airiness which she laments".[2]

There was nothing Ann enjoyed so much as writing about herself, and she has left us her autobiography in three parts, dealing respectively with her conversion, the special providences of God, and the publication of her books, to the number of about fifty. The autobiography is entitled *A Brief Account of the Gracious Dealings of God with a Poor, Sinful, Unworthy Creature,* the respective dates being 1743 for I and II, and 1750 for III. A "Letter" is appended, defending the right of a woman to print her message, notwithstanding that unfortunate saying of the Apostle's about a woman keeping silence in the churches ; the writer concludes with the remark that she can at least pray for those who will not read her.

Ann Williams was born in Northampton in 1692, brought up in a religious home, and attended the Independent Church at Castle Hill under the Rev. John Hunt (1698-1709). She blames herself for the early pharisaism which said, "I have been at Prayer, while others are at Play"—though it is doubtful whether she ever outgrew that fault. She was converted at thirteen by a deepened sense of the meaning of eternity, in glory or misery, and says, "I pray'd, read, heard in a very different Manner than I had ever done before". She records the thought, so illuminative of the pressure of Calvinism, "if I must go to Hell at last ; I desire I may be holy there". She was afraid to speak about her spiritual troubles to her parents, though her father sought to give her an opportunity. And so often the spiritual strain of these

[1] Whitley, *History of British Baptists,* p. 214.
[2] Whitebrook, *loc. cit.,* p. 132.

four months issued in physical breakdown, from which she was relieved by the potion of "a very skilful, tho' a very prophane Person". The peace that came through trust in Christ was disturbed by the thought "that all the Experience I had had of the Lord's loving Kindness was but mere Delusion" (we may compare the modern trouble about autosuggestion). Like Bunyan (whose *Grace Abounding* has influenced her narrative), the hero of the *Scarlet Letter*, and so many others, she is tempted to utter blasphemous thoughts and naturally does not know that this is but an inevitable psychological reaction from excessive religiosity. But she gains a true sense of faith: "I saw that believing was venturing, casting, trusting my Soul in the Hands of Jesus", i.e. an act of will, "a holy Venture" like Esther's. She recognizes that the experience of the saints may vary in particulars, though agreeing in general; the great thing is to "come as thou canst, tho' with a trembling heart". Prevenient grace was at work "in giving thee a new Nature before thou began'st to breathe after it". The note of genuine experience rings through all this, in spite of the stereotyped religious vocabulary and of the dependence on Bunyan and Rutherford.

The second part of the autobiography enables us to trace her outward movements, which are all more or less regarded as "special providences", and are specially linked to opportunities for worship and edification. It begins in 1709 with the removal of her minister, the Rev. John Hunt, and the succession of the Rev. Thomas Tingey (1709-29), whose ministry did not edify her, as she did not fail to inform him. She accordingly removed to the open-membership Baptist Church [1] in College Lane, then under the ministry of the Rev. John Moore, where she found "fat, green Pastures. . . . . The Sanctuary-Streams ran clearly; and the Sun shone gloriously. . . . . Mr. Moore was a great doctrinal Preacher: And the special Advantage I receiv'd under his Ministry, was the Establishment of my *Judgment* in the doctrines of the Gospel". Her *Brief Hints concerning Baptism* (p. 27) show that it was not till she was a member of College Lane that she was baptized on profession of faith (which incidentally shows the educative value of an open-membership Baptist Church

[1] *I.e.* a Church in which there *may* be membership on profession of faith without the requirement of baptism.

when the minister is, like John Moore, himself a convinced Baptist).

In 1714, at the age of twenty-two, she was married to her first husband, and this led to her removal to London, where she had communion with the Church at Cripplegate, under the ministry of the Rev. John Skepp. In the Cripplegate Church Book[1] there is a Register of letters, with an entry of date about 1715, "No. 18 Ann Catle from Northampton for Transient". This means that she was not fully transferred, but received into temporary communion, retaining her membership at College Lane. Her full transfer was made more than two years later, for we read in the Cripplegate book: "31st of the 1st mo. 1718. Same time one M^s Ann Cattle and M^s Martha Bass, members of the Church of Christ under the care of B^r Moor of Northampton, presented a letter of dismission to the Church which was read . . . M^s Ann Cattle gave a Large and very choice account of the Work of the Spirit of God on her soul to the great joy of the Church." Note the "Large"—very comprehensible to those who have waded through some of her writings. How Ann must have enjoyed herself on that occasion! She gives an interesting analysis and comparison of the preaching of Moore and Skepp; the latter went beyond the former in "Quickness of Thought, Aptness of expression, suitable Affection, and a most agreeable Delivery; . . . his Ministry abounded in Similies . . . the special Blessing I received under it was the more abundant Life and Power of the Truths known". Skepp's book on *Divine Energy* will explain this judgment; he left his mark on Ann, though her husband's business called them away for some time to Warwick. Here she found another climate: "I thought, when I came first, 'Surely, this People worship without the Blood of Jesus'. They stood at such a Distance from God in Prayer." She writes enthusiastically to Mr. Skepp that *he* does not "make a Composition of Matter, merely out of other Men's Judgments, and then commit it to a few dead Notes to read to the

---

[1] This is the Church Book which was the subject of the preceding study. Her husband's name is given by Mr. Whitebrook as "Coles", but this must be a mistake for "Cattell" or "Catel". In the College Lane Church Book, under date August 18, 1715, there is an entry: "Ann Cattell dismissed to Mr. Skepp's Church near Cripplegate in London."

People!" They soon returned to London, where, after five years (i.e. in 1719 or 1720) her husband died. She then returned to Northampton, and within a year or so married Benjamin Dutton, who had been apprenticed to a clothier and draper, had then studied for the ministry, and now, on their marriage, returned to his trade. She greatly missed Mr. Skepp's ministry, but after his death in 1721 transferred her spiritual affections to the Rev. William Grant, of Wellingborough. She evidently gave her husband no peace until they removed to Wellingborough, though this was long delayed for business reasons. There is an evident want of proportion when she compares herself with Abraham going out, not knowing whither he went, and with Ruth migrating to a strange land, for, after all, Wellingborough is only ten miles from Northampton. The fact that Mr. Grant was once "ill of a Quinsy" leads to pages of religious debate. She did not wholly exclude her husband from her anxieties, though we hear much less of him than of her favourite ministers. She was greatly upset when business kept him away three days beyond time, and had a great struggle to resist looking into the newspaper to see whether he was drowned—but that was not to be until a quarter of a century later. Finally, the Duttons got to Wellingborough, and Ann could listen to Grant on the Canticles to her heart's content. But again came disappointment. Business necessitated a removal to Whittlesey (near Peterborough), where her spiritual exile brought on an illness, during which she characteristically chose a text for her funeral discourse. We can see Ann, with her lively imagination, ecstatically imagining that scene as she lay in bed. Her friends decided (probably not without some prompting) that "it was necessary for me, for the Recovery of my Health, to return again into my own Air". They lived in Wellingborough for about three years, till in 1732 they removed to Great Gransden, in Huntingdonshire. This removal was not for business reasons. Mr. Dutton had been preaching for some time, and was now called to become minister of the Church there—a struggling cause. Her long debate as to whether she ought to go makes it plain that she regarded the call as one to herself even more than to her husband.

Her activity as a writer, already begun, formed her dominant interest in Great Gransden, to judge from the third part of her autobiography. This consists of a long and detailed account of the publication of her successive books. She is eager to tell both how she came to write them and how the way was miraculously cleared for their publication, even "in the Exuberance of His love, *Three at once*!" She speaks of herself as "a Favourite of Heaven, a special Favourite", and as one who "has a great name among some of [God's] children". She is specially eager that her books shall circulate in America, and when other matters take her husband to America, she enlists him as her distributing agent. Scripture is made to testify its confirmation of her desires at every point; thus the text "the Woman fled into the Wilderness" is a divine hint that her books would be used in the American Wilderness. She finds, of course, Scriptural warrant for an attack on Wesley's false doctrine, and Jael's example warrants a hammerblow at the Christians of Philadelphia. She calls her books her children ("How often have I admired divine Kindness, in that freedom from worldly encumbrances!"), and can thus appropriate the text "Leave thy fatherless children" for her MSS. But enough has been said to show, underneath the religious vocabulary, the kind of monomania which possessed this ambitious woman. Her husband remained in America from 1743 to 1747, and was drowned in returning. (Mr. Whitebrook rather unkindly suggests that he needed rest and peace.) It is a little startling to find that this extraordinary woman is partly comforted for his loss by the way being now open to the declining Church to get another minister! It ought to be said that she endowed the cause at Great Gransden, and "left the repute of a singularly patient, well-living old woman to survive her in the memory of friends who loved her".[1] Human nature is often a perplexing blend of many qualities.

The faults and limitations of the character thus revealed are obvious to all. Ann regarded her writings as a divinely directed means of evangelism, yet her spirit and attitude towards the great evangelists of the century is not unfairly described as "censorious",[2] We are conscious of the narrowness and provincialism of her outlook, her misuse of Scripture

---

[1] Whitebrook, *loc. cit.*, p. 140. She bequeathed her Bible to the only other notable woman in Baptist circles of the time, Ann Steele; it may be seen at Broughton (Whitley).

[2] Whitley, *op. cit.*, p. 214.

as a Delphic oracle to confirm her own desires, the unpleasant sentimentality of her use of Canticles, her conspicuous egoism. On the other hand, we ought to recognise that some at least of these faults belong to her age rather than peculiarly to herself. In spite of them, she is honestly seeking God, and trying to serve Him, and it is her misfortune that she belongs to a period and a religious circle of which the life has become artificial and self-absorbed. The moral of her story is drawn for us by history. The new life came through the new evangelism, liberated from outworn dogma, and the new duties which that evangelism inspired.

(7) A Baptist Student (John Collett Ryland)

William Newman, the first Principal of Stepney (Regent's Park) College, who was an assistant in the school kept by John Collett Ryland at Enfield, has told us [1] two incidents of John Collett Ryland's boyhood which may be taken as fully characteristic of him: "At twelve years of age he teazed his father so much for a gun that he knocked him down with a stick ; and then, to make it up with him, he gave him one. Soon after, as he was setting it down (not regarding the trigger) against a box, the whole charge went into the ceiling. After this his father gave him a horse. He bought spurs; and the faster the horse galloped the more he spurred him. At length the horse threw him against a bank, and left him there bleeding most profusely." This was the headstrong and passionate youth, born of an impetuous ancestry, who was captured for Christ and Calvinism by the young pastor of Bourton-on-the-Water, Benjamin Beddome. Here is what the youth wrote of his minister (in the diary which is the basis of this study[2]) when through Mr. Beddome's interest and influence he had reached the Baptist Academy at Bristol:—

June 25th., 1744. M 6½. Surely Mr. Benj. Beddome is an instance of the Existance of God and the Truth of the Christian Religion. Wt. Could Change his Heart, and induce him to leave his Profession or Trade—which was much more Profitable—and what could move him to Stay at Bourton rather yn go to Exeter, to which he was strongly sollicited—what is it yt moves him to

---

[1] *Rylandiana*, p. 2.
[2] Now in the Angus Library of Regent's Park College.

preach, Pray and be so active? is it not ye Delight he finds in ye Work—Tis plain that tis not Worldly Interest.

Here we see the aspect of religion which chiefly appeals to a young man—the unselfish and generous devotion to some high cause. Young Ryland was not so happy (or thought he was not) in the minister and teacher whom he found at the Bristol Academy, Bernard Foskett. Mr. Foskett, who also acted as minister of the Broadmead Church, won the enthusiastic praise of his colleague, Hugh Evans, for his character and devotion to duty during nearly forty wears of service ; but Dr. John Rippon, whilst quoting this praise, goes on to admit that " his method of education was limited rather than liberal ; severe rather than enchanting ; employing the memory more than the genius, the reasoning more than the softer powers of the mind ; . . . Mr. Foskett was not the first of tutors ".[1] So we find John Collett Ryland, eager and impetuous in temper, inquisitive and speculative in mind, rather discouraged by the training of this elderly disciplinarian who could not appeal to his pupil's enthusiasms: —

June 15. 2 in the Afternoon. If God dont bless me wth Abilities for ye Ministry I'll Get me a place to be an outrider for a Bristol, Coventry, or London Tradesman—when this year is finish'd with Mr. Foskett. I shall partly See how ye Matter will go—and if I dont Engage in ye Work of ye Ministry, I'll Endeavour to return ye Money Paid for My Board—and any More they Expended on My Account,—and what they Desire for Interest—and Engage in ye Business I served my Apprenticeship to Learn—and if Please God I am able I'll also Make Mr. Fosket a Handsome Present for bestowing his Pains on such a Dull Fool as I have been, and I am afraid shall ever be.

But the gratitude to Mr. Foskett here expressed gave way to other feelings. On April 1, 1745, after nine months' more experience of his teacher, he writes: —

This day when Mr. Foskett he chid me exceedingly—and spoke some Severe Words which make a lasting impression on my Soul. —but if he knew my desires and endeavours to approve my Self Sincere in the Presence of God, and the doubts I do—and have for a long time labour'd under—about some of the Fundamentals of all Natural and Reveal'd Religion—I believe he would not be so Severe in his Reflections upon me.

[1] *An Essay towards an History of the Baptist Academy at Bristol*, p. 22.

The next day, however, we read: "Mr. Foskett was in a good temper and us'd us kindly." That such an attitude should be chronicled suggests that it was the exception rather than the rule—which is rather hard on a college Principal! (Perhaps it is a good thing that students no longer keep college diaries.) A couple of months later (May 30, 1745) there is a rather enigmatic entry: "Note what Mr. B. Beddome told me last Saturday—that the Day before, i.e. on Fryday, Mr. Foskett *spoke to him again, about my going in the Country.*" Over this is written in specially large and distinctive characters, "Bernard Foskett's Ignorant Cruel Hardness of Heart to me". This unfavourable judgment of his tutor was no passing mood of indignation, for nearly forty years after (March 18, 1784, Thursday evening) John Collett Ryland wrote down this deliberate verdict on his college days: "Foskett should have spared no pains to educate our souls in grandeur, and to have enriched and impregnated them with great and generous ideas of God in His whole natural and moral character, relations and actions, to us and the universe. This was thy business, thy duty, thy honour, O Foskett! and this thou didst totally neglect."[1] That is a fairly sweeping condemnation, characteristic of the man who wrote it. Perhaps the truth was that the teacher's way of comprehending and handling divine truth was not the pupil's, and that the pupil was passing through his years of storm and stress, whilst the teacher had forgotten his own.

These spiritual struggles of a student's heart are reflected in not a few pages of the diary. Thus he writes (May 25, 1745), five days before the last-named entry: "I thought: If there was no God nor my Soul was not Immortal, no Death, Judgment, Heaven or Hell, yet I would not live beneath the Dignity of the Hunan Nature." Quite early in his college life he systematically analyses his condition:—

Inward man, for the most part, very dark, weak and wicked. My memory greatly failed me. My understanding very much blinded with sin. My conscience very stupid and unfaithful. My affections very carnal and corrupt. My reason almost ruined, and had little power to exercise itself. My thoughts exceedingly vain, corrupt and trifling, wild and ungovernable, unsteady and unfixed. Unbelief very strong indeed ; atheism, and every other

[1] Newman, *op. cit.,* p. 37.

corruption, working strongly in my heart. Sometimes ready to deny the being of God and of Christ, etc.[1]

Such condemnation of himself, in one form or other, constantly recurs throughout the diary. Introspective analysis is carried to an altogether morbid degree; wherever the fault may lie—with himself, with his college, with his theology—no one who reads these pages to-day could claim that he was taught to see life steadily and to see it whole. The seminary life can be as unhealthy as the monastic, and we are frequently reminded of the records of life in monastic communities by the diary of this Baptist student. Again and again he blames himself for having a good appetite for his meals, in such terms as these: "From 1½ till 2. Spent at Dinner: very greedy and after the Creatures. My rapacious appetite may well make me blush, and O! what Darkness, Atheism, Ignorance, Unbelief, Enmity, Madness, Distraction and folly, Selfishness and Uncharitableness Dwells within me in every Power of my Nature." (Feb. 15, 1744-45.) This morbidity was evidently reflected in his outward behaviour, for he records (Feb. 4, 1744-45): "Evg. at Supper. *Mrs. Heritage and Mrs. Evans gave me a hint about my strange, Stiff, unmannerly Conduct towards Mrs. Ev., and towards many of our Friends, etc. when I pass by them."* On the other hand, this shy and awkward youth from the Gloucestershire farm was apt to let himself go too much when it came to extempore prayer. Two days before this incident he writes: "Mr. Foskett gave me a hint to Day about expressions in Prayer—not to be too rash." The hint from the ladies evidently bore some fruit, for two days later we find the note, "God helping, Provide better for Table Conversation". Later (April 19, 1745) we find the resolution carried out: " This day at Dinner happily fell into a Strain of Telling remarkable Stories and Events—O! that I may be assisted to provide suitable, seasonable, pleasant, Profitable and usefull Entertainment this way, whenever I've an opportunity." He developed the methods of the expert *raconteur,* for farther on we read (May 13th): " The afternoon spent in finishing the Abstract, and in Collecting some little stories ; The evening after Supper spent in Reading and telling Little Stories." This facility in anecdote

---

[1] This is quoted by Newman, *op. cit.,* pp. 29, 30.

became quite a characteristic in the after-days, as his school-assistant, William Newman, records; one way of rewarding good conduct in the school was to fetch Mr. Ryland to tell a story. This is rather an interesting example of the way in which the consciousness of a defect may actually lead to the acquirement of a marked characteristic—when there is sufficient resolution. In Ryland's case that quality of resolution comes out most notably in what is known as the Bristol vow, which has often been quoted, first, I think, in the funeral sermon over John Collett Ryland preached by John Rippon in 1792 (p. 41). The original is written in large characters on a piece of worn and folded paper which has been pasted into the diary: —

June 25. Ev. 10—1744. Aet. 20 yrs 8 Months 2 Days.
If there's ever a God in Heaven or Earth, I Vow protest and Swear in God's Strength—or that Gods permitting Me, I'll find him out and I'll know whether he loves or hates me or I'll Dye and perish Soul & Body in the Pursuit & Search.
       Witness Jno. Coll. Ryland

Nobody but a thoroughgoing Calvinist, face to face with the definite issues of a limited Election and an alternative Reprobation, the love or the hate of God, could state the issue quite like that, and nobody but one of Ryland's eager, passionate, extravagant temperament could so fling himself into the search for God and ultimate truth. Yet the words do not rise to the noble height of that somewhat similar cry of Bunyan's, as he faced the prospect of death: " If God doth not come in, thought I, I will leap off the ladder, even blindfold into eternity, sink or swim, come heaven come hell. Lord Jesus, if thou wilt catch me, do; if not, I will venture for thy name." John Collett Ryland's strong Calvinism was proof even against Charles Wesley's eloquence. Under date April 2, 1745, we read: —

After meeting was over We went to hear Mr. Cha: Westley at the Room; he was preaching or expounding John 5, 1 to 14 verse, on Our Lord's healing the Impotent Man, and charging him to sin no more, Lest a worse thing should befall him. Mr. Cha. Westley positively asserted falling from Grace, in the strongest Terms. I thank the Lord I thought at yt Time on Mr. E. Coles Discourse on Final Perseverance, also coming home, and at Prayer and at

Supper, with an unusual Impression, and it seem's to Strengthen, Comfort and enlarge My heart in Thankfulness and Praise.

So the terrible heresy of Charles Wesley did him some service after all—by confirming him in his previous belief.

We get a glimpse of this student's meditations (quite unconsciously touched with humour):—

June 22d. Ev. 10. Laus Deo. I fell into a Beautifull Scheme of Reasoning as I sat Musing wth my head down and my eyes shut—Thus—How comes Man to be endow'd with those Various powers and properties wch I find in myself, viz.

I can cast my Eyes all around me in ye Day Light and see Coulers, Shapes, Motions. I can Look up and See the Sun with his cheering Rays in ye Daytime & ye Moon and Stars by Night, ye Sky, ye Clouds, etc.

Down upon this Terraqueous Globe I can see such a Sort of Beings as Myself, and also Females wch are some of them Sweet & Lovely Creatures, but who gave them & us of ye Male Sex our Existance ; Did We our Selves? No ; then we must be and not at the Same time.

Did our parents? No ; For wheres the Father or ye Mother yt will or Can Say that they—either Father and Mother Fashion'd their Sons or yr Daughters in ye womb. They neither of them knew wch Sex ye Child would be or wt. Shape, whether Strait or Crooked, Wise or Foolish, Ugly or Handsome.

To this interesting meditation there is appended the word " Unfinish'd ", and in that word much virtue lies. Elizabeth Frith, of Warwick, was probably not yet within his horizon.

No one could say, after reading this diary, that John Collett Ryland faced his life-work with a mean and impoverished conception of its intellectual demands. He drew up a most ambitious programme for a year's work at college.[1] It must be here sufficient to give another and briefer summary of his aims (June 7, 1744. M. 6¼):—

I beg if ever the most High God sends me forth into the Publick Work of the Ministry, I may go well Qualified, if it please his gracious Majesty to give me Large and Exact Skill in 5 Languages, and Large Skill and Knowledge of about 20 Arts and Sciences, Including that one which is above them all, viz. DIVINITY—this, this is what I would Excell in, Both in the Theory and Practice of Every Branch from the Greatest to the Least.

[1] Reproduced in the *Baptist Quarterly* for April, 1925.

He shows a very laudable ambition that he and his fellow-students may beat the college record, and "excell all the young Students that have ever been before us" (July 8, 1744). Already he cherishes thoughts of authorship, which he was destined to carry out almost too copiously. "N.B. Make a Little Greek and a Little Hebrew Gramr., if ever thou livest to have Skill enough" (July 10th). It is good to read that on going to bed on July 12th he "long'd to know more of the Hebrew Tongue". His methods of study are good, and his self-made "Rules for Daily Examination" might be profitably employed by the student of to-day:—

1. Wt New Words have I gain'd in the Eng. French, Latin or Hebrew Languages or in any Part of Grammar in those Tongues.
2. Wt. New Ideas in the Human Sciences. Especially Rhetoric, Logic, Ontology, History, Chronology, Geography or Natural Philosophy.
3. Wt. New Words or Ideas in evr'y Book that I have Read this Day, whether Human or Divine Subject.
4. Wt. Have I gain'd in Divinity either in ye Theory or Practice Part, in Keach, in Vincent, in Confession of Faith, in Dr. Ridgley's Body of Divinity, but more Especially wt have I gain'd from the Holy Scriptures Old or New Testaments.
And be sure Examine ev'ry night at Least; how much of Self has been in all thy Thoughts, words and works that Day, whether Natural, Sinfull, or Righteous Conduct (July 10, 1744).

He forms the excellent purpose of committing to memory select portions of the Bible, and tests himself by making himself repeat such passages whilst kneeling on his bed (July 3rd and 4th). He also constantly analyses the books he reads, and a good part of the diary is filled with such analyses. It may be of interest to quote in full a sample day from the diary, which shows him as an "introvert" and not an "extrovert" like Pepys, who was so full of zest for things without:—

Feb. 1. Friday. 1744-5. M. 6½ awoke. M. 7 arose, very dead, dark, hard and miserable. O! I am for ever Miserable, if Christ dont appear in rich Mercy to me. Pray'd & yn [then] read Genesis I.—at 7½ was call'd down to Breakfast & Prayer till 8¾; then came up Stairs; from 9 to 11 engag'd as usual; from 11 to 1, wth Mr. Foskett; from 1 till near 2 at Dinner; my heart too much engag'd in the Creatures, etc. ; from 2 to 4½, Putting my Papers & Books in good order ; very dark & dull all the time, tho' some Sorrow at bottom for my past sins and follies and present deadness & stupidity ; from 4½ down by the Fire, reading over my Quotidianas from June 16 to Dec. 31, 1744. Some things in them worth another Review—at 5 Begun Mr. John Reynold's Confirming Catechism—5th. edit. 12mo. 1734. About 6, Began his Book Entituled Enquiries concerning the State and Oeconomy of the Angelical Worlds.—8vo. 1723. A curious Treatise.—at 7 Began & took a Cursory View of it thro'out Mr. John Hurrion's Scripture Doctrine of the Holy Spirit, in 16 Sermons. 8vo. 1734. A Most Excellent & Glorious Performance. at 8 engaged wth our Family in Usual Service—and then till near 11, reading Mr. Hurrion's aforesaid noble Treatise.—O ! for a Heart to embrace this glorious Lord God the Spirit in all his Operations. ev. 11— up Stairs. Read as follows (viz) Promises To the Fatherless and Widow, pag. 45—Of the Means of Grace, page 77 to 81. To Faithful Servants.—Sect. 4. 202—Ps. I. Matth. 1—I thank the Lord I hope I had a little more Light to night. I hope God the Spirit has not quite forsook me—went to bed more Comfortable and Lively than for some time past—near 12 oClock.

It will be seen that the diligent student of those days got through an enormous amount of reading, including much more study of "theology" in the narrower sense than is done by the average student of to-day. If we ask how he found time for it, the answer lies in the story of such a day as we have just had. He concentrated on the one thing and had few distractions. We can count on the fingers of one hand the references to public events in the diary before us. There is no reference to social and philanthropic activities such as take no small part of the time and energy of a Christian man to-day. The sight of the "outsiders" in the streets of Bristol does not stir this young Calvinist to evangelistic or missionary ardour towards *them* ; he writes: "When out in Town, saw many poor objects—N.B.—God assisting Improve by them— and Stir up others—and constantly" (Mar. 30, 1745) ; or again: "N.B. this morning *going to Mr. Day I had such a sense of Distinguishing Goodness of God to me—above the 100ds & 1000s yt Walk about ye Streets that it exceeded my Belief. My Soul was almost overwhelmed at the Sense of it*" (May 8, 1745). There we have the unhappy side of the doctrine of predestination as held in the earlier part of the eighteenth century before the Evangelical Revival. We cannot forget that it is John Collett Ryland who opposed young

Carey's missionary enthusiasm so long after these Bristol days.[1] Ryland was an enthusiast himself, but then enthusiasts about different things always find it hard to understand each other. The truth is that the sharp cleavage between the Church and the world which is so well illustrated in this diary, and characterizes the religious life of the time, meant narrowness of judgment as well as concentration of aim. The faults that Protestants can see in Catholic asceticism have belonged often enough to Puritanism, which is indeed Protestant asceticism.

It would take us too far to trace the subsequent life and work of this young Bristol student, in his double capacity of Baptist minister and schoolmaster. The same characteristics remained, and the promise of his gifts and ardour was amply fulfilled. It must be sufficient to recall two passages to illustrate this. One is an account of the education of his son, John Ryland, who succeeded him as the minister of College Lane, Northampton, and afterwards became the Principal of Bristol Baptist College:—

> John is now eleven years and seven months old; he has read Genesis in Hebrew five times through; he read through the Greek Testament before nine years old. He can read Horace and Virgil. He has read through Telemachus in French! He has read through Pope's Homer, in eleven volumes; read Dryden's Virgil, in three volumes. He has read Rollin's ancient history, ten volumes 8vo. And he knows the Pagan mythology surprisingly. (August 28, 1764, as quoted in the funeral sermon by Rippon, p. 43.)

There is more than paternal pride in those words; there is the sense that he is giving to his boy that which he was once so eager to win for himself.

Better known is the story told by Robert Hall of his being taken by his father as a little boy to Mr. Ryland's school at Northampton. It was the time of the American War of Independence, and Mr. Ryland sided with the Americans against his own Government. Finally Mr. Ryland burst out characteristically with the declaration that if he were General Washington he would call for his officers and have them all bled into a punch-bowl, himself the first, and then all should dip their swords into the bowl, and solemnly swear never to

---

[1] See Chapter V, p. 113.

sheathe those swords whilst an English soldier remained in America. "Only conceive, Sir," said Robert Hall in telling the story, "my situation; a poor little boy, that had never been out of his mother's chimney corner before, Sir, sitting by these two old gentlemen, and hearing this conversation about blood. Sir, I trembled at the idea of being left with such a bloody-minded master. Why, Sir, I began to think he would no more mind bleeding me, after my father was gone, than he would killing a fly. I quite expected to be bled, Sir"[1] There we have Ryland of "the Bristol vow", still eager, passionate, extravagant, still young at heart in his enthusiasm. Whilst I do not attach much importance to "last words", I think that there is something appropriate in the last words of John Collett Ryland,[2] "I'll go and try."

(8) A Baptist Preacher (Robert Hall)

The "new boy" at Mr. Ryland's school was destined to become one of the foremost preachers of his time. Backward and weakly at first, he had learnt his letters in his nurse's arms from the gravestones of a burial-ground; later on this had been his study, whither he carried in his pinafore his little library, to lie amongst the long grass and quench his passionate thirst for knowledge. At nine he had read and re-read with keen interest Jonathan Edwards on the *Affections* and the *Will*, together with Butler's *Analogy*. After his school-days in Northampton he went, like his teacher, to the Bristol Academy as a scholar, helped by the benefaction of Dr. James Ward, and from Bristol to King's College, Aberdeen (1781-85), where (Sir) James Mackintosh was his inseparable student companion. He held pastorates at Bristol, Cambridge, Leicester, and again Bristol, where he died in 1831.

Here is the impressive description of his oratory by one of his Cambridge hearers who became his biographer:—

From the commencement of his discourse an almost breathless silence prevailed, deeply impressive and solemnizing from its singular intenseness. Not a sound was heard but that of the preacher's voice—scarcely an eye but was fixed upon him—not

---

[1] John Greene, *Reminiscences of the Rev. Robert Hall* (1832), pp. 93, 94.
[2] Newman, *op. cit.*, p. 22.

a countenance that he did not watch, and read, and interpret, as he surveyed them again and again with his rapid, ever-excursive glance. As he advanced and increased in animation, five or six of the auditors would be seen to rise and lean forward over the front of their pews, still keeping their eyes upon him. Some new or striking sentiment or expression would, in a few minutes, cause others to rise in like manner; shortly afterwards still more, and so on, until, long before the close of the sermon, it often happened that a considerable portion of the congregation were seen standing —every eye directed to the preacher, yet now and then for a moment glancing from one to the other, thus transmitting and reciprocating thought and feeling:—Mr. Hall himself, though manifestly absorbed in his subject, conscious of the whole, receiving new animation from what he thus witnessed, reflecting it back upon those who were already alive to the inspiration, until all that were susceptible of thought and emotion seemed wound up to the utmost limit of elevation *on earth*,—when he would close, and they reluctantly and slowly resume their seats.[1]

It is difficult, if not impossible, to recapture anything of this experience by reading the six solid volumes of Hall's collected *Works*. Their eloquence is stately and dignified, the vocabulary copious and well chosen, the intellectual mastery of the subjects treated very marked. But the style is that of a bygone day, and is too measured and elaborate for our modern taste, nor is the originality of thought sufficient to claim a permanent place in theological literature. To read the sermons is to be made conscious of the changing fashions of oratory and its inevitable dependence on the mental world and outlook of the hearers. Moreover, we must admit the criticism made even by his contemporary fellow-Baptist, John Foster, in a lengthy and searching characterization of Hall's preaching—that it was wanting in individualization, the direct and particular application to life, and dealt with man rather than with men.[2] We miss that power to see and represent the universal in the concrete particular which may make an ordinary sentiment memorable, and, in the copious wealth of Bunyan's imagination, creates literature. Yet Hall was a great figure of his day, a recognized genius as an

---

[1] *Memoir of Robert Hall*, by Olinthus Gregory, prefixed to vol. vi of Hall's *Works*. The biographical details of this study are drawn from the memoir; cf. also the brief sketches in the *Encyclopaedia Britannica* and the *Dictionary of National Biography*.

[2] This follows Gregory's Memoir in vol. vi of Hall's *Works*, pp. 143-88.

orator, described by an editor of his time as "perhaps the most distinguished ornament of the Calvinistic dissenters".[1] An Anglican contemporary, Dr. Parr, even compared him with Jeremy Taylor, as sharing "the eloquence of an orator, the fancy of a poet, the acuteness of a schoolman, the profoundness of a philosopher, and the piety of a saint".[2] His popularity is witnessed by the fact that the sermon on the death of the Princess Charlotte went into sixteen editions of a thousand copies each. His *Apology for the Freedom of the Press and for General Liberty* is quite in the Baptist tradition and attracted much attention; its denunciation of Pitt, beginning "A veteran in frauds while in the bloom of youth", leaves nothing to be desired in vigour.[3] Hall was prominent in a controversy within his own denomination as to the terms of communion with those who had not been baptized on profession of faith, his antagonist being Joseph Kinghorn, of Norwich. His own catholicity of outlook is seen in the protest against organizing a Church with a specific view to the propagation of some particular truth, which is, as he rightly says, a perversion of the original end and design of Christian societies. The result would be disastrous to truth:—

Every denomination will exhibit some portion of it, in a distorted and mutilated form; none will be in possession of the whole, and the result will be something like the confusion of Babel, where every man spoke in a separate dialect. As the beauty of truth consists chiefly in the harmony and proportion of its several parts, it is as impossible to display it to advantage in fragments, as to give a just idea of a noble and majestic structure, by exhibiting a single brick.[4]

There is, however, something more memorable than Robert Hall's oratory, and that is his undaunted courage and resolute character, in spite of extreme suffering. From early childhood to the very end he suffered more or less acute pain, which the post-mortem proved to be renal calculus. The surgeon who performed it writes: "Probably no man ever went through more physical suffering than Mr. Hall; he is a fine example of the triumph of the higher powers of mind exalted by religion, over the infirmities of the body".[5] To

[1] *Op. cit.*, vi, p. 132. [2] *Op. cit.*, p. 131. [3] *Op. cit.*, iii, p. 65.
[4] *Op. cit.*, ii, pp. 475, 476. [5] *Op. Cit.*, vi, p. 134.

the strain of this agony was doubtless due the mental breakdown of 1804 and 1805. A letter of April 11, 1805,[1] reflects the deep effect which this humiliation had upon him ; it is addressed to John Fawcett, one of the Baptist leaders in Yorkshire: —

I have undergone the severest affliction that ever befel me. The Lord has shewn me terrible things in righteousness. It has graciously pleased him, however, to restore my captivity, and to recover me to the perfect exercise of my reason. Assist me, my dear Sir, to magnify the name of the Lord. May a sense of the goodness of God be indelibly imprinted on my mind. Bless the Lord, O my soul, and all that is within, bless his holy name. I am a monument of astonishing mercy. May the goodness of God lead me to repentance and stimulate me to obedience.

It is significant of the man's sincerity that in the increasing paroxysms of pain towards the end his mind dwelt on the sufferings of Christ. He remarked to his doctor that " a contemplation of the sufferings of Christ was the best antidote against impatience under any troubles we might experience ; and recommended me to reflect much on this subject when in pain or distress, or in expectation of death ".[2]

Readers of Lord Lytton's novel, *The Caxtons,* may recall the fine tribute there paid to Robert Hall by a soldier who has read the memoir: —

What I have seen in this book is courage. Here is a poor creature rolling on the carpet with agony ; from childhood to death tortured by a mysterious incurable malady—a malady that is described as " an internal apparatus of torture " ; and who does, by his heroism, more than *bear* it—he puts it out of his power to affect him ; and though (here is the passage) " his appointment by day and by night was incessant pain, yet high enjoyment was, notwithstanding, the law of his existence." Robert Hall reads me a lesson—me, an old soldier who thought myself above taking lessons—in courage, at least.—(Part ix, chap. vi.)

[1] The manuscript is in the Angus Library of Regent's Park College.
[2] J. M. Chandler, *Authentic Account of the Last Illness and Death of Robert Hall,* p. 28.

III

BELIEVERS' BAPTISM AND THE EMPHASIS ON INDIVIDUAL EXPERIENCE

A RELIGIOUS community is never a merely logical or theoretical construction, based on and fully explained by a paper constitution. Like a State or any other form of continuous social life it is shaped on the anvil of history by repeated blows and varying temperatures, so that its distinctive nature emerges but slowly as the product of many factors. Thus the *emphasis* on believers' baptism which distinguishes Baptists is from one point of view an accident of history for which they are not responsible. It is due to the simple fact that others have lost a feature of New Testament Christianity which Baptists have kept. In this particular respect they are a projecting "shelf" on the rock of the Church, *because the other strata have "weathered"*.

(1) THE MEANING AND JUSTIFICATION OF BELIEVERS' BAPTISM

It is neither possible nor necessary to enter on a detailed examination [1] of the New Testament references to baptism in order to show that this was (*a*) the baptism of believers, (*b*) by immersion. So far as historical exegesis goes, these two points are usually conceded by competent scholars, as, for example, by Sanday and Headlam in their paraphrase of Rom. vi. 4:—

> When we descended into the baptismal water, that meant that we died with Christ—to sin. When the water closed over our heads, that meant that we lay buried with Him, in proof that our death to sin, like His death, was real. But this carries with it the third step in the process. As Christ was raised from among the dead by a majestic exercise of Divine Power, so we also must from henceforth conduct ourselves as men in whom has been implanted a new principle of life.—(*International Critical Commentary*, p. 154.)

[1] A fuller statement of this and the following paragraphs will be found in my *Baptist Principles* (Kingsgate Press, 1925), from which I have quoted some sentences in what follows.

Believers' Baptism seems to have been an invariable accompaniment, if not a definite sign, of entry into the Christian society.

It may, indeed, be argued that what was natural or inevitable for the first Christian missions ought not to be prescriptive for a Christian community in which children are brought into relation with the Gospel from their earliest days —or that the silence of the New Testament about the baptism of infants leaves us free to infer and to practise it—or that the difference of East and West, the ancient and modern world, warrants us in modifying the practice or dropping it altogether. But no one has the right to argue that the baptism of the *New Testament* is less than the immersion of intelligent persons, as the expressive accompaniment of their entrance into a new life of moral and spiritual relationship to God in Christ. It may further be argued that it is more than this, since the symbol in the ancient world usually carried an *effective* as well as a declaratory or expressive meaning, and to this point we shall return in the closing chapter. Christian baptism in the New Testament certainly means four great things, in the sense that these are its normal accompaniments. It implies a cleansing from sin; it is associated with the gift of the Holy Spirit; it is administered to believers and no others; and for Paul, at any rate, it meant an experiential union with Christ in His redeeming acts, deeper in meaning than words can express.[1]

We must distinguish quite definitely the *subject* of baptism (i.e. the believer) and the *mode* of baptism (i.e. immersion), for there can be no comparison of their importance for those who realize what New Testament faith means and are not mere literalists. The ancient mode may be defended on various grounds, especially that of its expressive character and its impressive influence; but if this were all, or even the chief point, there would be absolutely no justification for the existence of the Baptists. Nothing shows more clearly a failure to understand the faith of the Baptists than the frequent idea that they are a peculiar sect which insists on baptizing " adults " by immersion. They baptize not " adults ", but " believers " on profession of their personal faith in Christ, and this is their primary distinction, though it has a very

[1] E.g. Acts xxii. 16, x. 47, ii. 38; Rom. vi. 4.

important bearing on the constitution of the Church into which such believers enter by their faith; as a quite subsidiary point, they practise the most ancient form of baptism,[1] because they find this the most eloquent expression of the essentials of that faith—the death and resurrection of their Lord. As a matter of fact, it may be repeated that neither of the two kinds of Baptists, the "General" and the "Particular", at first practised immersion, so that the mode was historically, as well as logically, an afterthought.

We cannot here follow the historical development by which the Church gradually came to substitute the baptism of infants for that of believers.[2] A sentence by a quite impartial historian of dogma accurately sums up the facts: "Infant baptism, first demonstrable in Irenæus, still contested by Tertullian, was for Origen an apostolic custom".[3] Even so, it was not until the fifth century that infant baptism became a general practice.[4] That practice influenced and was influenced by many other developments of the life and thought of the Church which evangelical Christians deplore. In contesting it, Baptists are testifying against much more than an isolated and relatively unimportant custom; they are testifying against the whole complex of ideas of which it was a symbol, out of which grew the conception of the Church as primarily a great sacramental institution, administered by a body of officials vested with spiritual powers in which ordinary Christians could not share. We cannot, indeed, trace such testimony in the early centuries, and have therefore no right to infer its existence, but we do find believers' baptism practised among the Paulicians of the East about A.D.

---

[1] As is recognised in the rubric of the Anglican service, which prescribes immersion as the proper form of baptism, unless the child is certified to be weak. An amusing instance of confusion between the mode and the subject is recorded in connection with H. B. Swete. As a curate, he publicly baptized an infant by immersion. But this unheard-of act created a commotion in the parish, which led the old parish clerk to say, with grave shaking of the head: "Mr. Henry ought never to have done such a thing; that were believers' baptism" (*Henry Barclay Swete*, p. 27).

[2] See *Baptist Principles*, chap. ii: "The Abandonment of Believers' Baptism".

[3] Loofs, *Dogmengeschichte*, ed. 4, p. 212.

[4] On the other hand, the substitution of other *modes* of baptism for immersion is shown by the *Didache* to have begun at least as early as the first part of the second century, though immersion is there regarded as the preferable mode.

800, and amongst the Petrobrusians of the West in the twelfth century.[1] The practice also gave a name to the great "Anabaptist" movement of the sixteenth century, which extended over Europe, though here it was allied with a number of ideas and practices which have nothing to do with the principle which believers' baptism represents.[2]

It may be freely recognized that infant baptism, *considered apart from its historical context*, is a harmless and even useful rite, at least in *some* of its modern adaptations. In the significantly bare form of the *Book of Congregational Worship* the essential things are a promise by those who present the child that he shall be brought up in the nurture and admonition of the Lord, and a declaration of trust by the minister that "hereafter he shall not be ashamed to confess the faith of Christ". That is dedication at its simplest, and no explanation is offered of its connection with baptism, except for words borrowed from the Anglican liturgy, though hardly in the same meaning: "We receive this child into the congregation of Christ's flock." The same words appear in the Wesleyan order, with the addition "that he may be instructed and trained in the doctrines, privileges and duties of the Christian religion". The prayers for a change in the child's nature *follow* instead of preceding the act of baptism, and the emphasis falls on the covenant of the parents to be subsequently realized in the personal covenant to be made by the child when he comes to responsible years. The Presbyterian order emphasizes the doctrine that baptism is a sign and seal of the covenant of grace, which includes children as well as parents. Baptism is a divine pledge that God will fulfil His part in giving grace. All these types of teaching may be regarded as legitimate expressions of evangelical Protestantism, apart from their connection with a rite which belongs to believers only, according to the New Testament. The Anglican service takes us into a different realm, for it prays *before* the act of baptism, "sanctify this water to the mystical washing away of sin", and declares *after* the act that "this child is regenerate and grafted into the body of Christ's Church". The emphasis here falls on the actual activity of divine grace in water-baptism, not on the pledge of future activity. The underlying doctrine that baptism cleanses the

[1] *Baptist Principles*, pp. 53 ff., 57 ff.
[2] *Op. cit.*, pp. 59-64; cf. pp. 11, 12, of the present book.

child from the guilt of original sin (i.e. the sin involved in his descent from Adam), finds fullest expression in the canons of the Council of Trent, which frankly make baptism necessary to salvation. [1]

The common element in all these interpretations of baptism is the necessary *passivity* of the infant baptized. Whether baptism be called dedication, or covenanting by parents, or the sealing of a divine covenant, or an actual regeneration, it is throughout something done to, nothing done by, the baptized. So far as he is concerned, all of them are non-moral acts, though the act of the parents or sponsors is properly moral. The Baptist position is not simply a new phase of this succession of interpretations; it stands outside of them all as *the only baptism which is strictly and primarily an ethical act on the part of the baptized*. As such, it is the only type of baptism which is properly consistent with the logic of "Separatism" and the whole idea of a separated Church of believers. John Smyth, the first Baptist, saw this point when he said that "the Separation must either go back to England (i.e. the Anglican Church) or go forward to true baptism". A pædobaptist Separatist is always in unstable equilibrium, so far as this point is concerned. This explains why baptism falls into a relatively insignificant place, or drops out altogether, as it frequently does, amongst Congregationalists. The Baptist stands or falls by his conception of what the Church is; his plea for believers' baptism becomes a mere archæological idiosyncrasy, if it be not the expression of the fundamental constitution of the Church. We become members of the living Body of Christ by being consciously and voluntarily baptized in the Spirit of Christ—a baptism to which witness is borne by the evidence of moral purpose and character as the fruit of the Spirit.

But loyalty to the past is never an adequate ground for present usage, though many an abuse still stands upon it—to form the "slum property" of history. When a symbol ceases to have real and valid meaning, its retention can work nothing but mischief, such as a superstitious reliance on the mysterious as such. Our concern should be whether the

[1] At the other extreme, we find the total rejection of water-baptism by the Quakers; their attitude is that, as Robert Barclay says, "we do always prefer the power to the form, the substance to the shadow", and "we find not anything called the pledge and seal of our inheritance, but the Spirit of God".

symbol in itself and in its usage admits of such interpretation as would justify its continued use. What is the intrinsic worth of believers' baptism by immersion, apart from any question of loyalty to the original form and significance of the rite? What is there in this ceremony that makes it worth while to retain it, in terms of present moral and spiritual value? We may distinguish (1) its psychological value, (2) its emphasis on individual conversion, (3) its confessional value as the dramatic and efficient substitute for a verbal confession of faith.

Modern psychology has thrown into brilliant relief the importance of *acts* as influencing thoughts. "Actions speak louder than words." There must be some definite act to register and make memorable the experience of repentance and faith if they are not to become increasingly obscure and inoperative in retrospect. We live largely by memory, but memory depends upon landmarks. Hence the New Testament, with intuitive instinct, anticipates our psychology, and says: "With the heart man believeth unto righteousness; and with the mouth confession is made unto salvation."[1] Doubtless Paul is here referring to the confession of faith made in and with baptism. Now the baptism of believers asserts more emphatically than any words can do that which the believer also confessed at his baptism in words, viz. the repentance and faith, the conversion from darkness to light which is one half—the human half—of the meaning of baptism. It should be remembered that the apostle appeals again and again to the baptism of believers, especially in the sixth chapter of Romans, as the foundation of his moral or religious exhortations. "You know what you were then," he virtually says; "see what you ought to be now." Baptists alone in the Universal Church can make such an appeal to baptism, for to all other Churches baptism predominantly means something which can never be remembered by the infant. No really moral appeal to the grown man can be based on that which others did to him as an unconscious infant.

(2) The Importance of Conversion

The emphasis of believers' baptism on individual conversion is unmistakable. "Believers'" baptism does by contrast with the practice of other Churches emphasize a particular

[1] Rom. x. 10.

aspect of faith, viz. its individuality, its personal initiative, its consequent variety. By contrast—for if all Christian Churches had retained baptism in the Baptist way, the *distinctive* emphasis now characterizing Baptists would be lost (cf. p. 69). As it is, the Baptists are left to emphasize in a unique, though conservative, manner the individuality of Christian experience—a real truth, though by no means the whole truth. The one-sidedness of this emphasis (for which they are not wholly to blame) has had interesting results for their history and general development. It has inevitably accentuated the qualities of initiative and individuality. Baptists tend to be individualists in both thought and action. They claim liberty of thought for themselves, and on the whole have been ready to give it to others; they may co-operate amongst themselves for practical ends, but always with a reserve of individual freedom, and usually with a reluctance to delegate executive authority. We shall see that both the strength and the weakness of the Baptists may be traced to this emphasis on the individuality of their experience of God in Christ.

This emphasis on individuality may be specially seen in the place given to "conversion". Wherever conversion is taken seriously (as it must be when it is real), it is a lonely, because a unique, experience. John Bunyan (who was a Baptist, though of the broader type) has sometimes been foolishly blamed for the "selfish individualism" of his pilgrim, who started on his spiritual journey without wife and children. But it could hardly be otherwise. Within the same family group each member lives his own life, known or unknown to the rest. The modern "social emphasis", however laudable and necessary in itself, has tended to obscure the primary foundation of religion in the individual experience. A distinguished contemporary philosopher usefully and impressively reminds us that "religion is what the individual does with his solitariness". . . . "The great religious conceptions which haunt the imaginations of civilized mankind are scenes of solitariness: Prometheus chained to his rock, Mahomet brooding in the desert, the meditations of the Buddha, the solitary Man on the Cross—it belongs to the depth of the religious spirit to have felt itself forsaken, even by God." [1] It may be admitted, indeed it must often be urged, that personality is a

[1] Whitehead, *Religion in the Making*, pp. 47 and 19, 20.

much bigger thing than individuality, yet it certainly includes it. When we discover God, and respond to that discovery with any reality, it must be each for himself, however true it be that Christian conversion is always the discovery of others in God, others whose life is ours, for Christ's sake, others for whom we have become responsible. It is also true that conversion is a social outcome as well as a social inlet—that it is shaped and moulded by a thousand subtle influences and traditions passed on by the surrounding group, and that it is often directly linked with the adolescent stirrings of body and mind towards union with others. But all these things, to which the psychology of religion has devoted so much recent attention, are like the political and social and economic factors of the Reformation—they depend for their functioning on the vital spark of a personal, and therefore individual, experience of God.

It is not open to any well-informed man of to-day to treat conversion as an antiquated survival, an artificial "technique" of evangelicalism. The particular contents of any experience of conversion may be antiquated enough, for centuries of development may separate two men who walk along the street together. Again, it is easy enough to stimulate certain formal reactions by mass-suggestion and reiteration. But the comparative study of religion, in freeing us from the provincialism of ignorance about these things, has also shown us how universal and how significant in religion the experience of conversion is.[1] We must, of course, put aside the idea that conversion necessarily means a startling and dramatic experience. The favourite comparison in the Bible is with the dawn of light. But though there may be scenes in which "the dawn comes up like thunder out of China 'crost the bay", the normal dawn is gradual and almost imperceptible in approach, even if there will always be some significant moment at which the man could say, "Whereas I was blind, now I see". That awakening of human personality to the presence and power of the divine, however achieved, is of the greatest significance and importance. In this large sense of the term there must always be conversion in Christian experience, and the baptism of believers, marking (amongst other things) this crucial readjustment, is emphasizing that which deserves to be emphasized. Those who have assigned another meaning to

[1] See *Conversion, Christian and Non-Christian*, by A. C. Underwood.

baptism, yet agree as to the significance of conversion, sometimes become conscious of the lack of any significant expression of it in the institutions of their Church. They find that there is a real difficulty in getting one who is brought under Christian influence to register his experience through some definite and memorable act from which to make his new start. Unless this is done in some way or other the experience is apt to fade away. But where can we find a more impressive and memorable register of the birth of a new purpose than that which is provided by believers' baptism?

On the other hand, Baptists ought frankly to admit the tendencies of this strong emphasis on the act of decision. Just because believers' baptism has for them this primary significance, and is a unique act, expressing a unique experience, all that went before and all that comes after may easily become subordinate and secondary to a degree that is perilous. The normal convert is one who has grown up under the influence of the Christian home, the Sunday-school, and the services of the Church. Only where such influence is efficiently brought to bear on the growing life is the responsibility of the Church faithfully discharged. Many Baptists are conscious of a danger here, and the frequent use of the " Cradle Roll " in connection with the Sunday-school, and the increasing introduction of " Dedication Services " in connection with the Church, show them moving towards the fuller recognition of this responsibility. The danger subsequent to the impressive act of believers' baptism is that nothing, not even the Communion Service as usually conducted in Baptist Churches, seems comparable with it, and the baptized believer may easily come to think that the rest of his Christian life may be taken more or less for granted. Of course, ministers and teachers are always urging the contrary, and pointing out that believers' baptism is a beginning rather than an end, but the very frequency of their warnings shows that the peril exists.

(3) THE CONFESSIONAL VALUE OF BELIEVERS' BAPTISM

The confessional value of believers' baptism *by immersion* is that it becomes an " acted parable " (like the broken bread and the poured-out wine of the Communion Service) of the Lord's death, burial, and resurrection, which are the cardinal verities of evangelical faith and the historical basis of Christianity. The expressive acts by which the believer identified himself with Christ were accompanied, apparently, by the oral utterance of a confession of faith in its simplest form, viz. " Jesus is Lord ",[1] and baptism was into the name of the Lord Jesus.[2] Towards the close of the New Testament period this was expanded into the formula of baptism into the name of the Father, and of the Son, and of the Holy Spirit.[3] Later still, as is generally agreed, this simple confession was further enlarged into the Apostles' Creed (the baptismal confession of Rome) in the West and the Nicene Creed (the expanded form of the baptismal confession of Cæsarea) in the East. So far as the general substance and aim of these historic creeds are concerned, it may safely be asserted that Baptists are as loyal to them as are any of the evangelical Churches. Yet it is equally true that Baptists hold a very detached position in regard to creeds and formal confessions of faith *as such*. The only approach towards a creed held in common by Baptists[4] in this country is the " Declaration of Principle " in the Constitution of the Baptist Union of Great Britain and Ireland, which reads as follows: —

The basis of this Union is:

1. That our Lord and Saviour Jesus Christ, God manifest in the flesh, is the sole and absolute authority in all matters pertaining to faith and practice, as revealed in the Holy Scriptures, and that each Church has liberty, under the guidance of the Holy Spirit, to interpret and administer His Laws.

2. That Christian Baptism is the immersion in water into the Name of the Father, the Son, and the Holy Ghost, of those who have professed repentance towards God and faith in our Lord Jesus Christ who " died for our sins according to the Scriptures ; was buried, and rose again the third day ".

3. That it is the duty of every disciple to bear personal witness to the Gospel of Jesus Christ, and to take part in the evangelization of the world.

The student of creeds and confessions of faith will recognize that this is not a creed proper, as it makes no attempt to analyse and define the exact content of the Christian faith, but, as its heading says, a " Declaration of Principle ", expressing, as well as a brief statement can, the common ground of union on which the individuality of Baptist faith is left free to work itself out. The first clause posits personal

[1] Rom. x. 9 ; cf. 1 Cor. xii. 3.   [2] Acts viii. 16, xix. 5.
[3] Matt. xxviii. 19.
[4] Excluding " Statements of Faith " made by Free Churchmen in common.

loyalty to Jesus Christ as God manifest in the flesh for man's salvation. This, of course, excludes a "Unitarian" or "humanitarian" view of the Person of Jesus Christ. His authority over each believer is based on the divine character of His personality. But there is no attempt and no intention to frame a particular Christology, and each believer is purposely left free to interpret both the authority and its theological basis "as revealed in the Holy Scriptures", whilst each group of believers forming a Church of Christ is left free, within its corporate loyalty to Christ, to govern itself.

This may seem to afford no guarantee of what is usually known as an "evangelical" faith, for many heresies condemned by the Church in ancient or modern times might plausibly shelter themselves within such a declaration. The reason that Baptists are, generally speaking, homogeneous in their evangelicalism is to be found in the second clause, defining Christian baptism. There is here an implicit reference to the symbolical character of the baptism of believers by immersion, according to the teaching of Rom. vi., which Baptists regard as a charter of their distinctive faith and practice in regard to baptism. They find there a triple reference: (1) The historical facts of the death, burial, and resurrection of Jesus; (2) the symbolic reproduction of those facts in the actual going down of the believer into the water of baptism, his submersion, and his rising from the water; (3) the experiential parallel implied by faith in Christ, a spiritual union with Him in which the believer dies to sin and rises to newness of life. This, it may be said, is an ideal experience, never perfectly realized in any believer, not even in the Apostle who set it forth. But from this ideality comes the potency of the act for those who have been enlightened as to its meaning.[1] Every time such an act of Christian baptism takes place, the Pauline statement about the broken bread and the poured wine becomes equally applicable to the initial rite—"we preach the Lord's death until He come". Both the Supper and the Baptism in their different ways have an evangelistic function—they preach the cardinal facts on which

---

[1] We may say of it what William James has rightly said of the whole conversion experience, "that it should for even a short time show a human being what the high-water mark of his spiritual capacity is, this is what constitutes its importance" (*The Varieties of Religious Experience*, p. 257).

an evangelical faith rests, viz. the death and the resurrection of Jesus Christ. More impressively than by any verbal recital of a creed, the historical basis of *every* Christian creed is constantly brought before a Baptist Church. The cumulative effect of this repetition, even from a purely psychological point of view, must be very great. To this must be ascribed the general continuity of "evangelicalism" within the Baptist community. They are repeatedly brought face to face with the facts of the death and resurrection of Jesus Christ as the salient articles of their faith—an epitomized "Apostles' Creed". Yet, on the other hand, they are left free, indeed they are expected, to reach a personal interpretation of the meaning of those facts for Christian faith. They are guided to such an interpretation in the classes of instruction held wherever a Baptist minister faithfully discharges his duty. But they are not required to accept any form of words as the authorized statement of that interpretation. If this makes a high demand on personal intelligence (which is by no means universally satisfied), its very challenge is educative. The Baptist, moreover, is free from the embarrassment of ancient forms of words, which can no longer be held in their exact ancient meaning. He is committed to a living loyalty as the only adequate reproduction of the ancient faith. He is allowed full scope for the individuality of that loyalty, its necessary individuality if it is to be personal. Yet he is brought into personal relation with the essential facts of history, on which all Christian faith must build, if it is to keep its spiritual continuity. This—whether Baptists themselves always realize it or not—is the secret of that reluctance of Baptists to bind themselves by the historic creeds of the Church. They hold the contents of those creeds, it may safely be said, as loyally as any other body of Christians to-day. But they feel the peril of stereotyping that which must be living to be real, and the peril of substituting a formal assent for what is of value only as a personal conviction.[1]

[1] It is naturally difficult for those committed to formal creeds to realize that they are not indispensable, and may be replaced by an "atmosphere" which supplies health and vitality. I remember, when a student in Strasbourg, having a keen argument with a narrow-minded Lutheran lady on the one hand and a vehement Catholic Pole on the other, and I remember how impossible it was to make either of them understand the Baptist emphasis on a spiritual experience symbolized in believers' baptism, without the fetters of a rigid statement of its interpretation.

In the foregoing statement of believers' baptism I have said little of the motive which in practice appeals most powerfully to many Baptists, viz., the desire to obey a direct command of Christ (Matt. xxviii. 19) and to imitate His own acceptance of baptism at the hands of John (Mark i, 9, 10). I do not doubt (whatever be the date of Matt. xxviii. 19) that our Lord instituted the baptism of believers, but I believe it is in accordance with His spirit to emphasize the intrinsic meaning of the rite, rather than its extrinsic aspect as an act of formal obedience.

The third and remaining clause of the "Declaration of Principle" calls for notice here only as individualizing the responsibility of the Church for missionary work in the largest sense. As will be shown in a subsequent chapter, the consciousness of this responsibility is strongly developed amongst Baptists, and they are justly proud of their contribution to the evangelization of the world. It is not an accident of history that they have led the way in foreign missionary work ; it is a logical and obvious deduction from their emphasis on individual faith. The measure of personal conviction is seen in its vigour of expansion, its zeal of propagation.

IV

THE BAPTIST DOCTRINE OF THE CHURCH

THERE was something to be said for the old "Dissenting" distinction of the "Church", as the community of believers, from the "chapel", as the building used for worship by that community—a distinction by no means yet extinct. It kept the big name for the essential fact. It recalled the time when the Church was not yet the owner of useful property, and had no abiding city, yet was the Church. The change of terminology has come about inevitably through the need to counter the contemptuous use of "chapel", as though it were not the home of a true Church. But it remains necessary always to assert that men are more than things, and principles are more than utilities.

Let us try to imagine the different conceptions of "Church" in the minds of those who glance at some ecclesiastical building in a city street. To one man it is simply an architectural feature of the street in which he has no further interest (indeed, a landowner not far from London who had no church steeple in the landscape seen from his windows went to the expense of erecting a wooden one on a barn to satisfy his æsthetic instinct). To another man a Church is a survival from a past age of faith, maintained in the interests of a particular social group; it is a purely sociological phenomenon. To another it is chiefly a philanthropic agency, to be encouraged on purely practical and utilitarian grounds. Even those who bring a definitely religious connotation to the term "Church" from their own experience will often emphasize some relatively superficial feature in explaining the difference of one Church from another. What are the principles which Baptist Churches express?

(1) Membership and Polity

The Baptist Churches arose historically as a special development of Puritanism, and their conception of the

Church is a special form of the Puritan doctrine in general, when this had been passed through the sieve of "Separatism" (see Chapter I). The special feature is due to the retention of believers' baptism, with its emphasis on individual experience (see Chapter III). The most recent formal statement of the Baptist doctrine of the Church is that which formed part of the reply of the Baptist Union Assembly [1] to the Lambeth "Appeal":—

We believe in the Catholic Church as the holy society of believers in our Lord Jesus Christ, which He founded, of which He is the only Head, and in which He dwells by His Spirit, so that though made up of many communions, organized in various modes, and scattered throughout the world, it is yet one in Him.

We believe that this holy society is truly to be found wherever companies of believers unite as Churches on the ground of a confession of personal faith. Every local community thus constituted is regarded by us as both enabled and responsible for self-government through His indwelling Spirit, who supplies wisdom, love, and power, and who, as we believe, leads these communities to associate freely in wider organizations for fellowship and the propagation of the Gospel.

We reverence and obey the Lord Jesus Christ, our God and Saviour, as the sole and absolute authority in all matters pertaining to faith and practice, as revealed in the Scriptures, and we hold that each Church has liberty to interpret and administer His laws. We do not judge the conscience of those who take another view, but we believe that this principle of the freedom of the individual Church under Christ has the sanction of Scripture and the justification of history, and therefore we cannot abandon it without being false to our trust. Moreover, it is plain to us that the headship and sole authority of our Lord in His Church excludes any such relations with the State as may impair its liberty.

Here the three paragraphs respectively declare (1) the diversity in unity of the Catholic Church of all believers, (2) the right of the local Church to be self-governing, (3) the sole authority of Christ within the Church. These claims are explicitly based on the principle that the Church is a society divinely controlled, and implicitly on the assumption that the "Congregational" polity here stated is adequate to the operation of that divine control. It is always the implicit assumptions of such a statement that need most carefully

[1] At Leeds on May 4, 1926.

watching, because those made explicitly are usually common ground. All who belong to the Christian Church in any recognizable form would assert the *ultimate* Headship of Jesus Christ over it ; the point that needs discussion is not this, but its implications and the manner in which it is conceived to be administered. It is these assumptions and implications which are so hard to express because they make the real life of the community.

Let us take the normal and typical " convert " who proposes to " join " an English Baptist Church. He has probably passed through the Sunday-school; he may not have received definite religious instruction from his parents, possibly not Baptists. He has joined a Bible-class because one of his friends took him, and for the same reason he comes, more or less, to the Sunday services. Perhaps he also belongs to the Society of Christian Endeavour or a Young People's Guild. He feels he wants something to live for and something to live by, and all around him there are people suggesting that this something may be found through faith in Jesus Christ. He may often lack clear ideas as to what such " faith " means, but he has enough confidence that Jesus Christ is a true Leader of men to put discipleship to the proof, and he responds to the appeal of his teacher or minister, and says he wants to be a Christian. He goes to the minister's Preparation Class, held from time to time as there are candidates for baptism, and receives some instruction as to Church Membership and Discipleship, Baptism, and the Lord's Supper, in which the minister will follow no prescribed form.[1] His name is brought before the Church, the report of " visitors " on his fitness for fellowship is heard, and a vote taken. Finally, he comes forward with others to profess Christian faith in baptism, and is admitted into Church Membership[2] by being given the " right hand of fellowship "

---

[1] It must be frankly acknowledged that this duty is often neglected by ministers. I once asked a class of twenty students how many had received what they would now call adequate instruction in Baptist principles, and found that seventeen had not, though some of these had heard occasional addresses on the Baptist faith.

[2] Entrance into the Church is regarded as distinct from baptism, though in practice usually combined with it. Believers' baptism is not infrequently administered to Christians of other communions, who have no intention of joining a Baptist Church.

at the next observance of the Lord's Supper. He is now expected to attend the monthly Communion service, to be regular in attendance at the services, to make some regular contribution to the funds of the Church, if he is earning a living. He is encouraged to take up some form of Christian service, such as Sunday-school teaching. He will depend for further instruction in the faith on the sermons or addresses he may hear. He will go to the Church Meeting from time to time, where he will be called upon to give his vote on matters which the "deacons" bring before the Church. He may eventually become a deacon himself by the election of the Church, one of a committee which virtually manages the affairs of the Church, though always with theoretical reference to the directions and judgment of the whole Church. By such apparently "casual" paths a man is brought to face the highest issues.

Our young friend thought he was "joining" the Church; he may awaken to the much more serious discovery that he is helping to "constitute" it—that the Church, according to Baptist faith, is not a hierarchy of officials, with an appendage of laymen, but a society of men and women drawn together by common convictions and needs, and entering into a social experience of the Christian faith for which their individual experience has so far prepared them. It is possible, of course, to say that this conception of the Church lacks dignity and fails to elicit reverence adequate to its true idea. In practice that may be perfectly true; the outer form and the inward idea are always tending to react on each other, and the idea is the more malleable of the two. It *is* difficult to keep the august and majestic conceptions of the Epistle to the Ephesians alongside of the friendly and natural intercourse of the first disciples with one another and with their Lord. Yet it should always be remembered that the Church grew out of human fellowship and friendship, and that it is never true to its origin when it ceases to be in some sense a family. The worst type of Baptist Church is that in which this human side of the relationship has somehow been lost, but fortunately such a Church will extinguish itself and cease to exist. Where there is real and helpful fellowship, even though there is a lack of reverence and a certain superficiality in regard to deeper truths, we have at least one vital element of the Church of the New Testament pattern.

It will be seen how entirely the spiritual efficiency of such a Church as this will depend on the quality of the individual convictions on which it rests. In the days of clear-cut Calvinism there was a definite body of religious doctrine with which everyone started, together with a certain neglect of what seem to us not less definite social duties. To-day there is usually the practical desire to be of use in the world along the lines of Christ, and a good deal of indefiniteness as to doctrine, or at least a very superficial response to it. But in itself the principle of a regenerate Church is sound, when we allow for the inevitable conditions of a union of "body" and "soul". "St. Paul's conception of a Christian community is a body of which the Spirit of Christ is the soul."[1] As Christ by His Spirit makes a temple of the individual body, so Christ by His Spirit may make a temple of the collective society. The society is a larger opportunity for the activity of the Spirit of God. That activity, however, is not guaranteed by a society any more than by an official or group of officials.

The idea underlying the congregational polity of a Baptist Church could still be sufficiently expressed in the words of Dr. Joseph Angus: "The Christian Church is founded on the double principle, that all true religion is a personal thing, and that the Churches of Christ are associations of religious men—of all such and of none besides."[2] But the four-score years since those words were written have brought some considerable changes to all the Churches. It is no longer possible to "prove" the case for a particular form of polity by a string of Scripture texts. For one thing, our general attitude towards the Bible has changed or is changing. It betokens no lessening of reverence and loyalty towards the moral and religious ideas of the Biblical revelation to say that the *forms* of its life are not necessarily those most suited to the needs of to-day. Indeed, we have no right to assume that these forms were ever intended to be authoritative for all time. They are experiments rather than precedents; they show life active and vigorous, creating its own means of expression as each need arose. Why, then, should we stereotype one particular stage in the development, whether it be early or late? Moreover,

---

[1] Lindsay, *The Church and the Ministry in the Early Centuries*, p. 69.
[2] *Christian Churches*, p. 70 (1863).

even from the earliest times there are the germs of many later developments. It is perhaps historically true to say with Lindsay that " we see a little self-governing republic " in such a Church as that at Corinth[1]. But, on the other hand, the authority of the Apostle Paul is very real, and is firmly exercised ; he is far from being the self-effacing chairman of a democratic society. The modern study of the New Testament has taught us to see more and more clearly that the emphasis falls on the life of the Spirit creating these transient forms rather than on the forms themselves. It is not sufficient, therefore, to prove that there were Congregationalist or Presbyterian or Episcopalian forms of Church government in the New Testament times ; the previous question must be faced—what authority, if any, have these forms over the present life of the Christian Church? Against those who insist on organization as of the essence of such a Church it is perfectly legitimate to argue that the gathering of the Upper Room was a fellowship rather than an organization; on the other hand, is there any valid reason, other than practical convenience, why the Church in Jerusalem should be "independent" of the Church in Antioch? The whole issue seems to be transferred from the theoretical to the practical—what is the best and most efficient way of expressing that conception of the Church which we hold to be true?

The conception of the Church as a society of believers is assuredly no unworthy one, nor is it lacking in majesty and dignity for those who know what faith means. Faith is a spiritual adventure, a challenge of the seen in the strength of the unseen. Christian faith in its simplest expressions always implies the great underlying unities of all the Churches, " one Body and one Spirit, even as also ye were called in one hope of your calling ; one Lord, one faith, one baptism, one God and Father of all, who is over all, and through all, and in all ".[2] It argues a poverty of spiritual imagination when we fail to see in the human temple, individual or social, a worthier sanctuary than any material shrine. We may say that the ideal of a society of holy believers is never fully and adequately realized in men and women of flesh and blood, but this is a quite different thing from saying that the ideal

[1] *Op. cit.*, p. 57. [2] Eph. iv. 4.

itself is wrong or inadequate. Newman asks in one of his books "what there is venerable, awful, superhuman in the Wesleyan Conference to persuade one to take it as a prophet". Certainly nothing is venerable or awful or superhuman that plays fast and loose with history [1] but where two or three are gathered in the name of Christ, and therefore with His promised presence, who is the Truth, there is ample room for veneration and awe and faith in the supernatural guidance of those two or three, even though they be no more than a village prayer-meeting. "Where Christ is, there is the Church." John Smyth could say of his little group of fellow-believers, in replying to a contemporary:—

> If you knew but the comfort and power of the Lord's ordinances of admonition and excommunication as we do (blessed be our good God) in some measure, and that growth and reformation which is in some of us thereby, you would be so wonderfully ravished with the power of God's ordinances that you would acknowledge the Church to be terrible as an army with banners, and yet amiable and lovely, comely and beautiful.—(*Works*, ii, pp. 441, 442 ; quoted by Burgess, *op. cit.*, p. 91.)

Baptists hold, then, that the congregational polity of a Baptist Church is one legitimate way amongst others of expressing the fundamental idea of the Church.[2] The theoretical centre of its activities is the "Church Meeting", usually held monthly. Here all members of the Church are at liberty to speak on matters affecting its common welfare, but the control of the meeting is naturally in the hands of the "deacons" and the minister, who presides. These usually form an Executive Committee, with a good deal of variety in the powers assigned to them, so that in practice they often become a sort of "Kirk-Session"; indeed, it might be argued that in a really efficient congregational polity it is necessary that they should. The deacons combine, however, the spiritual functions of "eldership" with the financial functions of the diaconate in the Presbyterian Church (though many Baptist Churches have a separate Finance Committee). In

---

[1] As when Newman speaks of the Virgin Mary as going to Mass (*Discourses to Mixed Congregations*, p. 356).

[2] Many Baptists, perhaps a majority, would not be content with this statement; they would urge that because it is nearest to the historical beginnings of the Church it is the form obligatory upon us.

the seventeenth and eighteenth centuries the Church Meeting was largely concerned with matters of "discipline", i.e. the faith and conduct of its members. No one with any capacity for human sympathy can turn over the pages of one of these old Church-books without feeling the tragedy and the comedy of it all—the vision of a great principle and not infrequently the misinterpretation of that vision for want of any true perspective.[1] This little group of men and women of whom we may be reading is so very much in earnest, so authoritative in its interpretation of Scripture, so fearless in the application of its authority, that we cannot but be impressed. Yet we feel also that it *is* a little group, divorced from the life of the great world about it, and inevitably to have its faith modified when that world is taken into full account. This is what has happened to English Baptists as to other religious communions of the Free Churches. Discipline has necessarily been relaxed, for no religious community could make such demands on the attendance or even the conduct of its members as were made in the seventeenth century; many Baptists think discipline has been relaxed beyond what is right or reasonable. In practice, discipline is now confined to grosser moral evils; a Baptist Church would not tolerate sexual immorality or habitual drunkenness or proved dishonesty in business relations in any of its members. Such cases are dealt with by personal investigation, usually by the minister and deacons, by private remonstrance or appeal, by suspension of membership for a time, until there is credible evidence of true penitence, finally by exclusion from the fellowship of the Church. Formal suspension and exclusion naturally require the vote of the Church, but in practice voluntary withdrawal is often counselled by the minister to avoid scandal.

Except for the more critical moments in the history of a Church, as when a call to a new minister has to be given or some change of general policy or activity introduced, the Church Meeting at the present day tends to become an ordinary service, differentiated only by the fact that "the minutes of the former meeting were read and confirmed". Many Baptists are seriously troubled by this frequent decline

---

[1] Examples have been given in the historical sketch contained in the second chapter (pp. 43-49).

in the place given to the Church Meeting, since it is the pivotal centre of the Church consciousness and gives the really distinctive character to a Congregational polity. The decline is partly due to the rivalry of other forms of organization, started with the best of intentions—Christian Endeavour Societies, Young People's Guilds, and the like, together with the very large number of special organizations not linked to any one Church, yet drawing their supporters almost exclusively from the Churches. The truth is that the Baptist of to-day has a great many other interests, religious and secular, which lie outside the circle of the Church, to a much greater extent than even the Victorian Baptist. His conception of the relation of the Church to the Kingdom of God has subtly changed, for he no longer identifies them in the way Baptists (like their fellow-Puritans) once did. The Kingdom of God is inevitably seen to be much larger than the Church, with many " values " for life which the Church consciousness does not touch. This is probably one of the main factors in the present drift from all the Churches, at least so far as serious-minded people are concerned. There seems no remedy for it but to widen the conception of Christian activity until it includes much more of life. The very phrase " Christian worker " calls up a narrow and impoverished picture of some two or three types only—the district visitor, the Sunday-school teacher, the secretary of some religious organization. But Christian service is being rendered by every Christian, in whatever vocation, who applies his faith to the affairs of his daily occupation. It is just this practical service which the Church has allowed to pass beyond its horizon, to its own great detriment. I do not see any prospect of a revival in the Church Meeting, which means in the Church consciousness of Baptists, apart from such recognition of the work of the Kingdom in a larger sense and of the leadership of the Church in the work of that larger Kingdom. An ideal Church Meeting of to-day would be one in which member after member of the fellowship spoke of the helps and hindrances of his daily life in the light of great Christian principles—in which the Christian magistrate and the Christian lawyer, the Christian manufacturer and the Christian shopkeeper, the Christian typist and the Christian errand-boy, all pooled their Christian experience for the common good, and learned to think of themselves as being

Christian workers and what they did as Christian work.[1] Our ecclesiastical theory and practice have not kept up with the changes in our practical philosophy. Our outlook on life as men and women is bigger than our outlook as Baptists or Wesleyans or Anglicans. Who does not feel something of that in reading a denominational newspaper?

The self-governing independence of the local Baptist Church obviously does not, and ought not to, preclude some sort of voluntary association with other Baptist Churches. From the beginnings of Baptist Church life in the seventeenth century right on to the present day successive forms of organization have been evolved to meet new needs, though the independence of the local Church was always jealously guarded and explicitly recognized. No one can understand the life of the denomination who does not realize that all larger groupings of Baptist Churches are for common action by representatives, not for the exercise of authoritative control. The local Churches join or withdraw from these as they see fit, though in practice there is stable union and a large measure of joint activity. Baptist Church life is thus expressed in three stages of representation, which indicate a growing world-consciousness and the sense of larger problems. The first grouping is that of the " Associations ", of which there are 30 in England, 14 in Wales, making with the Unions of Scottish and of Irish Baptists a total of 45. These Associations usually include smaller local groups, which need not concern us ; it is the grouping of the county (or practicable area) which forms the first effective unit beyond that of the local Church.[2] Each Association carries on its own denominational life in its own way, though there is naturally an increasing tendency to assimilation. A President is elected

[1] Cf. the address by Professor Barry on " The Holy Spirit in the Church ", delivered before the Church Congress at Southport, October, 1926: " Religion to-day is, in the large, simply one activity side by side with all the others, not standing even in vital relation to them. Religion is ceasing to be the inspiration of life's best ideals and activities, and obviously that spells a double loss. They are losing their quality and ' saltness ', and religion itself is left thin and bloodless, with no strong roots and spreading out into life. The Churches as we know them to-day are mainly *devotional* associations ; they are not fellowships of life and work." (The address is given in full in the volume *The Eternal Spirit*, edited by Canon Raven, pp. 116-136.)

[2] The earliest of those now existing is the Bristol Association (from 1640).

annually, very often a layman, and the annual meetings of the Association (usually held near Whitsuntide) form the centre of its ecclesiastical year. Almost all of these are in membership with the "Baptist Union", the second kind of grouping. This was first formed in 1813, though it did not become of much importance for the next eighteen years. Its "Assembly", meeting annually, is constituted by representatives of the Baptist Churches in voluntary membership with the Union, together with personal members (whose voting power is conditional on the consent of the rest). Such an "Assembly" is naturally too large to deal with any but the broadest issues of policy, and in practice the direction of common interests is in the hands of the Council of the Union, consisting of 165 members, elected partly by the Assembly and partly by the Associations. (There are, of course, a large number of special committees.) The President of the Union is elected annually, and a layman frequently fills this office, as with the provincial Associations. There are upwards of 1,500 Churches in membership with the Baptist Union. There are as many more of one sort or another remaining outside in the exercise of their freedom, though the main stream of Baptist Church life flows through the Baptist Union. About 600 Churches, unable to pay their ministers the minimum salary of £160, are helped to do this by the "Sustentation Fund". In connection with this, and for other purposes also, the country is divided into ten Areas, with a "General Superintendent" in charge of each, but the name must not be taken to imply more than moral and persuasive authority. It would quite misrepresent their position and work to regard them as "bishops"; but they are more than travelling secretaries. They are encouragers and advisers, and are at the service of the Churches and ministers for all spiritual purposes.

In 1905 a further step in representative organization was taken by the formation of the Baptist World Alliance, which has held its Congresses in London, Philadelphia, Stockholm, Toronto, Berlin and Atlanta. Its latest returns show about ten millions of (communicant) members, eight and a half millions of these belonging to North America.[1] There are over 72,000 Baptist Churches, over 51,000 pastors and

[1] See Appendix III.

missionaries, and upwards of eight million Sunday scholars. Baptists form, therefore, one of the largest of the Protestant Churches, indeed the largest Free Church communion in the world. This fact is a remarkable testimony to the vigour of the ideas they express, especially when we remember the lowly beginnings of Baptist Church life in the seventeenth century, the absence of social or political support, and the presence indeed for a long time, and even now in some countries, of social and political repression or persecution. The organization of American Baptists follows the same general principles, as may be seen from the following statement: —

We have the district Associations or voluntary assemblies of messengers from local churches covering a limited district. We have our State Conventions, which include messengers from all parts of the State, and our general conventions among English and continental and other Baptists. Our organization, therefore, in its amplitude and geographical extent is equal to that, say, of our Presbyterian brethren, but without imitating them in the introduction of the principal of indirect authority. None of these bodies is legislative or judicial. Christ is the sole authority in all. They are for advisory and administrative purposes.

Then, too, our superintendents and secretaries of missions perform the work of bishops without any of the authority of bishops. They visit the fields and lend a helping hand by means of suggestion and in other ways. But they have no semblance of authority over any congregation, however small. We have also a great variety of Boards and Councils. Congregationalism is capable of great diversity in this respect. These are not rigid in form that they may not be changed when occasion arises. Thus there is all needful flexibility.[1]

(2) Worship

An Anglican, entering a Baptist Church for divine worship, might often be alienated by the seeming want of reverence. There is no visible altar, and an obtrusive pulpit takes its place. The choir is too visible, and does not seem greatly concerned with anything but its own function. Deacons walk about unnecessarily, and even come to chat with people in the pews. The secretary gives out notices at an alarming length, and may intersperse a few remarks. The preacher, who wears

[1] Mullins, *The Axioms of Religion*, pp. 147, 148.

no distinctive dress, follows no particular order in his prayers, and may be wearisomely long in his sermon. People stay about in clusters talking when the service is over, and the minister may come down and join them, or stand in the vestibule shaking hands with people. As for the Communion Service—— !

There is some truth in this impression, though not as much as is imagined. It would be better for Baptists to cultivate more reverence in the forms of worship, and to think more intelligently about the meaning of those forms, since thought and feeling are always being shaped by their own expression in deed as well as by word. It is all too easy for those who protest against a fixed ritual to slip into a pseudo-ritual of their own, slipshod and provincial, instead of dignified and comprehensive. Yet it must be remembered that the Church is a family as well as a building or a body, and that the vital warmth of human fellowship can be sanctified to high spiritual ends. Even if some of these people talk when it would be better for them to be silent, or err unconsciously in matters of taste, yet the weightier matters of Gospel fellowship may be theirs. The Church is their spiritual home in a real sense, with all the "homeliness" of familiar association. The many organizations and activities of the week provide human fellowship for them and their families. Whilst the increase of these for special objects has, as we have seen, its unfortunate side, in depriving the Church Meeting of part of its significance, we must not fail to recognize that these various activities provide an outlet for energies in useful employment, and, above all, provide opportunities for Christian fellowship in the wider sense of the term. We may admit, as I think Baptists ought to admit, that there is something wanting on the side of reverence in our expression of worship, but we ought also to claim that a very real side of Church life does find expression in this homely fellowship.

What are the ideals of worship which ought to control the practice of the Baptists, given their general standpoint and conception of the Church? The fundamental fact in all worship is the bringing of the soul face to face with God ; in this sense, as William Penn says, "worship is the supreme act of human life". Calvin began his "Institutes" by the words, "Almost the whole sum of our wisdom, which ought to be reckoned true and solid wisdom, consists of two parts, the knowledge of God and of ourselves ". Newman tells how early Calvinistic influences acted upon him, " making me rest in the thought of two and two only absolute and luminously self-evident beings, myself and my Creator ".[1] A. M. Fairbairn, in a brief study of worship which is one of the best expressions of the Free Church ideals,[2] says: " Worship in its fundamental idea may be said to be the speech of God to man and of man to God. . . . Where the specific Christian elements appear is in the quality and character of the beings related."[3]

The new feature of " public " worship as compared with private devotion is the corporate and collective quality, which introduces no alien element, since sociality is as much an attribute of personality as individuality. We are what we are because we have grown up in a society, from the earliest influences of the home. When men come together for a common purpose that unites them, their powers for that purpose cannot be reached by the arithmetic of mere addition of the units ; they are a new unit, whether it be a political meeting or a religious service. As the players in an orchestra must learn to limit themselves, yet thereby are able to reach new results—which the composer can achieve only through their combination—so for ourselves and God corporate worship opens new possibilities. Both in common praise and in common prayer—the two elements of such worship on the human side—the individual gains something new by the subordination of his individuality to the social thanksgiving and petition.

The forms which worship ought to take are ruled by no authoritative principle, save that of the Apostle, " Let all things be done decently and in order, for edifying ", i.e. " building up ", man's conscious relation to God. The development of the centuries has naturally been from simpler to more elaborate forms. The primitive Christian meeting followed the synagogue rather than the temple, and was controlled by what has well been called a " liturgy of the Spirit ".[4] From the subsequent elaboration of Church worship Protestantism returned to more democratic forms,

---

[1] *Apologia*, p. 4.
[2] *Studies in Religion and Theology*, pp. 253-82.
[3] *Loc. cit.*, p. 264.
[4] Duchesne, *Origines du Culte Chrétien*, p. 48.

especially in the Puritan movement. Early Baptist worship is described for us as it was carried out in Smyth's Separatist Church in Amsterdam:—

> We begin with a prayer, after read some one or two chapters of the Bible; give the sense thereof and confer upon the same; that done, we lay aside our books and after a solemn prayer made by the first speaker he propoundeth some text out of the Scripture and prophesieth out of the same by the space of one hour or three quarters of an hour. After him standeth up a second speaker and prophesieth out of the said text the like time and space, sometimes more, sometimes less. After him, the third, the fourth, the fifth, etc., as the time will give leave. Then the first speaker concludeth with prayer as he began with prayer, with an exhortation to contribution to the poor, which collection being made is also concluded with prayer. This morning exercise begins at eight of the clock and continueth unto twelve of the clock. The like course of exercise is observed in the afternoon from two of the clock unto five or six of the clock. Last of all the execution of the government of the Church is handled.—(Letter of Hugh and Anne Bromehead, given in Burgess, *Smith, the Se-Baptist*, etc., pp. 170, 171.)

It will be observed that there is no singing, even of psalms, in this order. But, as was shown in an earlier place,[1] Baptists became pioneers in congregational hymn-singing. In modern times the chant and the anthem (not always to advantage) have followed the hymn, and there is an increasing tendency to break up the "long prayer" into shorter and more intelligibly followed petitions, though there is no general movement amongst Baptists towards a liturgy which would displace this "free" prayer.

To this prayer and praise the divine response may be conceived to come in three ways—in the reading of Scripture, which is the record of man's experience of God through many centuries, and has proved its power to recreate that experience in new settings; in the sermon, whether expository of the meaning of Scripture, or "prophetic" as the utterance of the preacher's new experience of God or outlook on contemporary life (both becoming the vehicle of the Spirit of God, "a hammer that breaketh the rock in pieces" on lines of cleavage prepared by the Providence of God); and in the

[1] See p. 48.

third place, the voice of the Spirit may sound in uncovenanted ways, through the incidental phrase of hymn or prayer, through the cumulative effect of worship, when custom is vitalized, as in the synagogue of Nazareth, into one of its rare moments, or in the unspoken message of the Spirit: —

> . . . the breath
> Of God in man that warranteth
> The inmost utmost things of faith.

God is Spirit, and worship is free to choose whatever forms may best lift men into the realm of the Spirit, since all forms, whether of Jerusalem or Samaria, are subordinate to the reality of that inner experience of God's presence, which is worship in spirit and in truth.

(3) THE COMMUNION OF THE LORD'S SUPPER

"The ordinance of the Lord's Supper", or "the Communion Service", is generally observed in English Baptist Churches monthly, after the first evening service of the month, though many Churches also observe it after one of the morning services for those who find this more convenient. The choice of name is characteristic; "the Lord's Supper" implies that it is the commemoration of the simple meal in the Upper Room, whilst "the Communion Service" implies that it is an act of fellowship—the fellowship of believers with one another and with their Lord. This is the justification of the place assigned to it in the present book. For Baptists the Lord's Supper is the supreme expression of the fellowship of the Church as created by, and maintained in, the fellowship of individual believers with Christ. They believe that special significance for all time was given to the last meal of which Jesus partook with His disciples, through His own words and actions, and that He made the broken bread and the poured-out wine the symbols of His body to be broken on the Cross, and of His blood sacrificially outpoured, in the manner of the symbolic acts of Hebrew prophecy. That which the word more clearly articulates the deed more graphically presents.

This primary conception of the Lord's Supper makes it a close parallel to the rite of believers' baptism, another "acted parable" when by immersion. The unrepeated act of baptism is the rite of initiation, the repeated act of communion that of continuation, in the community of believers, but both proclaim the Lord's death. Dr. Denney's impartial statement has a special significance for Baptists: "Modern Christians try to draw a broader line of distinction between the Sacraments than really exists. Partly, no doubt, this is owing to the fact that in our times baptism is usually that of infants, while the Supper is partaken of only by adults, whereas, in New Testament times, the significance of both was defined in relation to conscious faith."[1] Those who practise infant baptism, with any serious doctrine of baptismal regeneration attached to it, are quite logical in following this up, as they sometimes do, with a "Children's Eucharist". On the other hand, Baptists approach the Lord's Supper in the light of believers' baptism as neither more nor less requiring personal faith for its benefits to be enjoyed. Thus the two ordinances illuminate and reinforce each other.

The Lord's Supper becomes, in the first place, a pledge of fidelity renewing the vow of loyalty made personally in baptism. The honour of the Lord's guests is pledged by their continued and repeated presence at His Table. They are bound to come in humble penitence, asking the pathetic question of the first disciples, which is so characteristic of a truly sacramental hour. When Jesus spoke of unfaithfulness in their midst, they did not resent the charge with Petrine indignation. Their hearts were too much subdued; they were brought too close to the sorrowful possibilities of human nature, under the solemn influences of the farewell. They could not look at others asking, "Is it *he*, Lord?" They looked at their own hearts, saying humbly, "Is it *I*?" It seems fitting that the first act in the Communion Service should be a confession of sin and a prayer for pardon.[2]

The elements employed in the two rites are complementary in their spiritual symbolism. The water of baptism is the symbol of moral and spiritual cleansing; the bread and the

---

[1] *The Death of Christ*, p. 136.

[2] But for a general service there is truth in Martineau's criticism of the Prayer Book order: "The profound sense of sinful imperfection is not ready on the surface of even the humblest mind; and it is not till the spirit has felt its way through the mists and dimness in which Prayer begins, and emerged into the clear presence of the Infinite Holiness, that the abasing consciousness of spiritual poverty is awakened, and the sad interval is seen between what we are and what we ought to be" (*Life and Letters*, i, p. 383).

wine are the symbols of moral and spiritual support. But the reality set forth is in both rites the work and gift of the Holy Spirit. Without His presence and activity, sanctifying the obedience and the manner of it, creating that fellowship of faith which is, as the Benediction implies, His peculiar work, there can be no sacramental communion. Fellowship means activity on both sides, and the fellowship of God in Christ with man is always mediated by the Holy Spirit. It is fitting, therefore, that at the Communion Service we should offer such a prayer as the *Epiclesis* of the Eastern Church, an invocation of the Holy Spirit.

The Lord's Supper expresses the spiritual unity of the Body of Christ, that Body into which believers are baptized in one Spirit. As they are made one by baptism in one and the same Spirit, so they renew that consciousness of unity in the acts expressive of the fellowship of the Spirit. It is fitting, therefore, that we should offer prayer at the Communion Service for "the communion of saints" and give thanks for those departed who still belong to the general assembly and church of the first-born.

The interpretation of the Lord's Supper most common amongst Baptists at the present time would be technically described as "Zwinglian"—though it must be remembered that there was a recognition of mystical union with Christ in Zwingli's teaching which did not find full expression in his controversies. There have always been Baptists whose interpretations of the Lord's Supper is Calvinistic rather than Zwinglian, and there is to-day a growing consciousness that this rite has not taken the place amongst us which belongs to it, and that it should be celebrated with greater reverence.

Whilst the Communion Service is fundamentally a memorial rite—"This do in remembrance of me"—it is much more than this for all who receive spiritual blessing through it. It renews obedient loyalty, and it establishes and mediates fellowship, both with God in Christ and with fellow-members of His Body. It implies the real presence of the risen Lord by His Spirit, and Baptists might join the great theologian and humble believer, Richard Hooker, in saying, "The real presence of Christ's most blessed body and blood is not, therefore, to be sought for in the Sacrament, but in the worthy receiver of the Sacrament" (V, lxvii, 6).

Baptists have no prescribed form of Communion Service, as they have none for baptism or for worship in general.[1] But the words of institution are always read, prayers are offered, and the elements are distributed by the deacons to the communicants. Any member of the fellowship, permanent or temporary, may conduct the service, but in practice the minister almost always presides. A voluntary offering for the poor of the Church is always taken at the regular Communion Service, and this is afterwards distributed by the deacons. The attendance of Church members is recorded by a ticket system, which enables those absent to be noted and visited.

The relation of believers' baptism to the Lord's Supper raises an issue on which Baptists are divided, i.e. as to whether the communion of the Table should be "strict" (in the sense of being confined to those who have been baptized on profession of their faith) or "open" to believers in general. The issue has been argued at much length, as between Kiffin and Bunyan, representing the "strict" and the "open" position in the seventeenth century, between Booth on the narrower and Robinson and the Rylands on the broader basis in the eighteenth, between Joseph Kinghorn and Robert Hall in the nineteenth. For the greater number of British Baptists the issue is now practically settled. At the beginning of the nineteenth century Robert Hall could write: "Strict Communion is the general practice of our Churches, though the abettors of the opposite opinion are rapidly increasing both in numbers and respectability."[2] At the beginning of the twentieth Charles Williams could write: "Charles Haddon Spurgeon, with the majority of British Baptists, invited all who loved the Lord Jesus Christ to commemorate with them His love in dying for them."[3] That result has come about by the larger logic of the essential unity of the Church over against the narrower logic that a man is not fully a Christian

---

[1] The order of service outlined above is rather more detailed than that of most Baptist ministers. It begins with a hymn, is followed by (1) prayer of confession, (2) invocation of the Holy Spirit, (3) words of institution and prayer of thanksgiving, (4) distribution of the elements, (5) prayer for the communion of saints, followed by the collection for the poor of the Church and a closing hymn.

[2] *Works*, ii, p. 16.

[3] *The Principles and Practices of the Baptists*, p. 25 (1903).

unless he has been baptized according to what Baptists regard as the New Testament baptism. To exclude a fellow-Christian from the Lord's Table does seriously reflect on the quality of his Christianity.

The question of "strict" and "open" communion at the Lord's Table should be clearly distinguished from two other issues with which it has frequently been confused. It has nothing to do with the doctrinal difference between the "Particular" or Calvinistic and the "General" or Arminian Baptists, though the combination "Strict and Particular" has been common. Neither has it anything to do directly with the further question of "closed" or "open" membership of the Church. This concerns the requirement of baptism by immersion as a condition of entrance into the Church. The great majority of Baptist Churches throughout the world are in this sense "closed" to any but believers baptized on profession of faith. But there are a number of English Baptist Churches which allow membership on profession of faith without baptism. It would certainly be a curious result if the practice of "open" membership should become as predominant amongst Baptists as that of "open" communion. Our dictionaries might then define a Baptist Church as the only one which did not make baptism a condition of admission! But the issue is hardly to be settled by the analogy of the open-communion question. The Lord's Supper is the Lord's gift to the Church; it lies outside our jurisdiction in a sense in which the administration of the affairs of a local community does not. It may be regarded as a matter of expediency rather than of principle that other Christians not personally pledged to the practice of believers' baptism should share with Baptists in the administration of a Church. Under the present constitution and polity each Church is entitled to judge for itself as to what is expedient, whilst equally the majority would be justified in refusing to recognize as a Baptist Church one in which the testimony to believers' baptism ceased to be effective. It cannot be denied that there is a certain peril in the increase of open-membership Churches (though the peril is not so great as it might seem, provided the minister is himself a convinced Baptist). It may also be argued, as is done by American Baptists generally, that clear-cut testimony is always more effective than compromise.

(4) MINISTRY

As the Lord's Supper expresses the fellowship of the Church in its dependence on Christ, so the "ministry" denotes the service rendered within and through that fellowship for Christ's sake. " Pastors are, in a word, the servants of the Church. The Church, indeed, is not their master; but they are, nevertheless, its servants."[1]

In any statement of the nature and function of the Christian ministry which is based on the New Testament principles and practices there are certain questions of historical exegesis which meet us on the threshold, and to which a definite answer must be given. Does the New Testament insist on any *form* of ministry at all? Does the emphasis fall on *office* or on *gift*, and how are they related? Is the later "monarchical" bishop the product of elevation or localization—is he, for example, an exalted presbyter or a settled apostle? Finally, what does apostolical succession mean, in the light of the earliest history of the Church? Obviously there can here be no argued discussion of these themes, on which so many volumes have been written, and they are named only to bring out the essential Baptist position, which finds support in the critical scholarship of all schools. That position is an emphasis on the inner, spiritual, and intrinsic nature of Christian ministry, its particular forms being accidental and occasional, evolved to meet particular needs as they were felt, such as the ministry of the seven at Jerusalem.[2] The ministry was richly varied in its contents, ranging from the itinerant work of an apostle to the word of exhortation spoken by the member of a local Church, yet it was regarded in all its forms as a "gift" of the Holy Spirit.[3] The office grew out of the gift, and not vice-versa. Paul, for example, became an apostle because, as he tells us, " God thought well to reveal His Son in me ".[4] Against the theory that Christianity is " the establishment of a visible system of means for realizing the end of human life ",[5] and the statement that " All authority was concentrated in the upper room of Pentecost. Thence it has been devolved ",[6] it is sufficient to point out that the natural

---

[1] Angus, *Christian Churches*, p. 47; cf. 2 Cor. iv. 5.
[2] Acts vi. 1-6.   [3] 1 Cor. xii. 4-11, 28-31; Eph. iv. 11 ff.
[4] Gal. i. 15, 16.   [5] Gore, *The Church and the Ministry*, p. 313.
[6] Lacey, *Unity and Schism*, p. 127.

meaning of "they were all together in one place" includes the hundred and twenty disciples who have just been mentioned, as well as the Apostles, and to say, with the Bishop of Gloucester, that the Apostles "represent 'discipleship' in its highest form . . . they are not primarily the appointed rulers of the Church, but the nucleus of the Church out of which it grew".[1] As for the evolution of the monarchical episcopate, the general principle framed by Bishop Lightfoot (apart from particular theories of its operation) seems to have stood the test of the searching criticism to which it has been exposed, viz. that "the episcopate was formed not out of the apostolic order by localization, but out of the presbyteral by elevation".[2] In regard to apostolical succession, there is truth in this, so long as we are speaking, with Irenæus, of the succession of witness to true doctrine, or of the performance of apostolic functions, such as discipline and teaching. But when it is defined by Bishop Gore as "in each generation an authoritative stewardship of the grace and truth which came by Jesus Christ and a recognized power to transmit it, derived from above by apostolic descent",[3] it is sufficient to let one bishop answer another, in the statement of Dr. Headlam: "So far as I am able to judge it was not held at all in the early Church. I have, I think, read everything from the Fathers which is quoted in favour of Apostolic Succession, and I do not know any passage which speaks of succession by ordination in this sense."[4] In fact, as Dr. Macgregor well puts it, the true successors of the Apostles as witnesses of Christ were not men, but the Four Gospels.[5] He puts our alternatives clearly and forcibly when he asks: "Is the ministry of the word to be a dragging chain, with link holding simply by the next link, and thus, through saints and reformers and prophets and apostles, coming at last to the throne of God? or does it at every stage depend on God

---

[1] Headlam, *The Doctrine of the Church and Reunion*, p. x. So also Hort in his *Christian Ecclesia*, p. 30, where he reminds us that the Lord's Supper was given to the Apostles alone, yet admittedly was meant for the whole Church: "The Twelve sat that evening as representatives of the Ecclesia at large; they were disciples more than they were Apostles."

[2] Essay on "The Christian Ministry", p. 196 (in *St. Paul's Epistle to the Philippians*, ed. 1898).

[3] *Op. cit.*, p. 59.   [4] *Op. cit.*, p. 128.

[5] *Christian Freedom*, p. 186.

directly, on a Divine call and Divine instruction and Divine illumination by which alone the instructions can be understood?"[1]

In view, therefore, of the New Testament evidence, the Baptist feels amply justified in refusing to make any distinction between "clergy" and "laity" which implies a difference of status and privilege and not simply a function and service. In the wide sense of the New Testament, all Christians are called to minister, according to their "gift"; whatever they are able to do for the service of the community and of the world they are called to do. The ministry of "laymen" in this sense is fully maintained and jealously asserted amongst Baptists; there is nothing which a "minister" in the professional sense is called upon to do—preaching, administration of the ordinances of baptism and the Lord's Supper, the conduct of Church business, the performance of the marriage ceremony, the burial of the dead—which a "layman" as such is debarred from doing.[2] This clear principle, recognizing intrinsic gift instead of extrinsic office, is in no wise contradicted by the fact that Baptists have found it expedient to institute a more or less "professional" ministry, equipped by special qualities and training for the usual performance of these duties. But in the earlier Baptist generations there was no such professional ministry. As Dr. Whitley, writing of the period 1640-60, says:—

Baptists put in practice the priesthood of all believers, and had no paid ministry released from the discipline of ordinary life. In the country, the typical minister was a thatcher, a farmer, a maltster, a cheese-factor; in the town, the preacher had been during the week making shoes, pins, buttons, collars, hats, clothes, had been dyeing or upholstering or selling such wares; here and there might be found a scrivener, a writing-master, an apothecary, even a doctor. As the ministers rode to their Association meetings, like Canterbury pilgrims, the butcher and the baker were joined at least by a candle-maker and an ironmonger; they would change horses at a post kept by a Baptist post-master minister, and would be entertained by a brother shipwright or carpenter. The score of ex-clergy were lost in the multitude of common men who ministered to their fellows,

[1] *Op. cit.*, p. 194.
[2] There is a "Lay Preachers' Federation", but the use of lay preachers is not nearly so wide or so organized as amongst the Methodists.

speaking out of an experience they shared with those they addressed. The priesthood of all believers was illustrated on a new scale.—(*History of British Baptists*, pp. 96, 97.)

Such authority as these men naturally came to exercise in their office was derived from the community which (acting as it believed under the guidance of the Holy Spirit) called them to exercise it. The principle could not be better stated than as it is given at the very beginning by John Smyth:—

We maintain that the power of the Eldership (i.e. the ministry) is a leading, directing, and overseeing power, ministry, or service, in the Kingdom and Priesthood of the Church, and that the negative voice, the last definite determining sentence, is in the body of the Church whereto the Eldership is bound to yield, and that the Church may do any lawful act without the Elders, but the Elders can do nothing without the approbation of the body or contrary to the body."—(*Paralleles*, p. 440.)

Presumably the legal definition of a Baptist minister in the full sense at the present day would be one whose name appears in the current list of the *Baptist Handbook* as duly accredited. Behind this official recognition there are three stages, viz. (1) a credible vocation, the consciousness of a divine calling to this particular form of service ; (2) either a collegiate training in a recognized institution or a prescribed course of study tested by examination, together with some practical experience of the ministry during a probationary period ; (3) the external corroboration of the inner call by the invitation of a particular Church to become its minister. This has been formally expressed by the Assembly of the Baptist Union as follows:—

By the *Ministry* we mean an office within the Church of Christ (not a sacerdotal order) conferred through the call of the Holy Spirit and attested by a particular or local Church.

By *Ordination* we mean the act of the Church by which it delegates to a person ministerial functions which no man can properly take upon himself.[1]

There is no prescribed, or indeed very uniform, order for ordination, but there is an increasing desire amongst Baptists that it should be a solemn religious service, and not, as too often it has been, a public meeting devoted to personal

[1] Annual Assembly of April 24, 1923.

eulogies. The resolution just quoted wisely continues: " It is recommended that the ordination, or any subsequent induction service, should include the observance of the Lord's Supper." This is the more fitting, because the primary conception of the Supper amongst Baptists is that it expresses the fellowship of believers. It is within, not above, this fellowship that the minister is set apart for the service of all. His best work will be done through ordinary human intercourse with his fellows; he must draw his motive for it from that high motive of constraining love which the Lord's Table sets forth; he must live on that high level of spiritual life which is made possible alone by the nurture of the Holy Spirit, symbolized in the elements; he must find his primary evangelical message in the Cross which the Table commemorates. In regard to the test of vocation, few tasks are more difficult and responsible than the selection of candidates for ministerial training. So many different qualities are required in a Baptist minister, and success depends on such a happy combination of these qualities, that no simple formula can be framed. Baptist individualism is carried into the ministry as into other realms of thought and action, with the result that a great deal is left to personal initiative and freedom. The student for the ministry is trained to think, but is encouraged in most of our colleges to think out his own system of truth; he is trained to act, but in the spirit of Wellington's remark, "the secret of success consists in the application of good sense to the circumstances of the moment and at the moment". The essential qualities are conviction, sympathy, and that rather mysterious forcefulness and distinctiveness which we call "personality". Approval by a college selection committee is provisional, and does not guarantee admission into the Baptist ministry. A further test of vocation is found in the confirming call of the

---

[1] It has been my own practice, when conducting ordination services, to give an explanatory address to the ordinand and the Church on these lines, then to ask the ordinand to kneel at the Communion Table for the Ordination Prayer with the "laying on of hands" in which it is desirable for a representative of the Church and of the whole denomination to take part. The "laying on of hands" is a New Testament rite of identification, which does not imply (except for Simon Magus) any magical transference of power; cf. Acts vi. 6 and xiii. 3. But Baptists have largely forgotten its frequency in their earlier days, and are therefore often needlessly suspicious of the practice.

local Church and the approbation of the early years of work by the Association to which the Church belongs. In recent years the Assembly has found room on its too crowded programme for a brief service of recognition of ministers passing from the probationary to the fully accredited list ; this usefully reinforces the corporate relation, which has not been adequately recognized.[1]

[1] The Baptist minister is supported by the voluntary offerings of the particular Church which has invited him ; endowments are rare and small and do not seem to be without peril. On the other hand, from various funds, the whole denomination makes grants to poorer Churches, to enable them to bring up the normal stipend paid to the minister to a minimum of £250, with allowances for children (the minimum for an unmarried man is £208). A denominational Superannuation Scheme was adopted in 1928.

V

THE MISSIONARY SPIRIT OF THE BAPTISTS

THE great prophets of Israel transformed the idea of God by interpreting it in the light of moral conviction and social duty. In their ethical passion they either flung down the barriers of nationalism or left such gaps in them that they ceased to be barriers for all true successors of the prophets. The discovery of a duty is the salt of religion; the implicit universalism of morality is certain to make itself explicit and to demand a corresponding universalism of religion, wherever there is room for true expansion. It is significant that a modern Jewish scholar should criticize Jesus for His ethical emphasis: "He both annulled *Judaism* as the *life-force* of the Jewish nation, and also the nation itself as a nation."[1] It is no accident that the foremost figure of the New Testament after Jesus should be not an ecclesiastic but a missionary, and that his chief difficulty should be with the nationalistic spirit of Judaism. The Christian faith is essentially a missionary faith, for it is faith in a God who deals with men in terms of their common humanity and leaves no room for the limits of nationalism or ecclesiasticism or sectarianism, save as these may minister to the more inclusive reality. Thus the missionary spirit is always a test of Christian conviction. It is true that we cannot reverse this, and say that where there is propagating zeal there is the Christian conviction of a world-gospel, because many other motives may lead men to become zealous proselytizers. But it is also true that no man can sincerely share the New Testament faith without desiring and seeking its expansion throughout the whole world. The measure of loyalty to the King is passion for the Kingdom.

We could not draw a faithful picture of Christian life in the New Testament times which ignored its essentially missionary character. The foreground is occupied by men who were first of all missionaries. In the Gospels Christ is the centre

[1] *Jesus of Nazareth*, by Joseph Klausner, p. 390.

of missionary activity; we see Him sending His disciples to the cities and villages of Israel. The very name "apostle" is eloquent of this vocation of the first disciples; they were men "sent off" to preach the Gospel. The Acts of the Apostles, the first of all Church histories, is really the record of the missionary labours of Peter and Paul in widening circles of appeal. The Epistles of Paul are the letters of a missionary to his converts, largely concerned with the practical problems of missionary work, but for which they would never have been written. The seer of the Apocalypse lifts his eyes from the Churches of Asia, creations and centres of missionary activity, to the unnumbered multitude out of every nation before the throne of God, and hears already that future song of praise to the Lamb repeated from the ends of the earth. But there is something to be seen which is even more impressive than the evangelistic energy of these protagonists of the faith. In the background of the picture we get frequent glimpses of unknown men and women, engaged in the ordinary occupations of life, yet not less earnest in their evangelism than their greater brethren. Their names for the most part are not enrolled in any book written on earth, yet to them, rather than to any apostle, the proud Church of Rome must ascribe its origin. A group of such names is found in the closing chapter of Paul's letter to the Romans, most of them being otherwise unknown to us. Yet it is clear that these unknown men and women were all of them living centres of personal evangelism, men and women who "laboured much in the Lord", men and women whose houses were often the homes of Churches. It is the spirit of personal evangelism which is the genuine missionary spirit, and all *forms* of missionary organization are subsidiary to this, whilst the usual appropriation of the adjective "missionary" to *foreign* missionary work is as much to be deplored as the parallel appropriation of "Christian worker" to a quasi-professional class of Christians.

A significant feature of this earliest evangelism was its naturalness and spontaneity. It moved along the lines of normal human contacts with an unstudied and untutored simplicity. Jesus Himself takes life as it comes, and uses the apparently casual opportunity—by the well, under the tree, on the cross. Paul sings hymns in prison or says grace on the reeling deck of a storm-tossed ship, and these are as much a part of his evangelism as the speech at Athens, and perhaps more influential. Aquila and Priscilla are eager propagandists, and their migrations from Rome to Corinth and from Corinth to Ephesus illustrate the trade relations and movements which had so great a part in the evangelization of the Empire. Trade followed the flag, or rather the Roman eagle, and Christianity followed trade, as a good map of the distribution of early Christianity will show. The movements of the centurion's party of soldiers guarding Paul remind us that a Christian soldier would naturally become a travelling missionary as his century or legion moved from place to place. We note Paul's hint about the possible influence of a Christian husband or wife on a heathen partner, and the letter to Philemon shows how the relation of master and slave could be evangelized. In fact, Celsus makes such personal evangelism the ground of bitter accusation:—

We see, indeed, in private houses workers in wool and leather and fullers, and persons of the most uninstructed and rustic character, not venturing to utter a word in the presence of their elders and wiser masters; but when they get hold of the children privately, and certain women as ignorant as themselves, they pour forth wonderful statements (*Origen against Celsus*, iii, 55, trans. of A.N.C.L.).

The faith of the Baptists claims to be a return to the primitive simplicities of the New Testament, and in theory and practice has tended to repeat these features of the early days of Christianity. Their early ministers were laymen, as we have seen; their early missionaries and evangelists were themselves. It is instructive to take a typical case of such personal evangelism, which shows us how genuine conviction tends to propagate itself. Between 1790 and 1795 a youth named John Wheeler left his home on a Gloucestershire farm to make his way in the world. He found work in Northampton in a tallow-chandler's shop and attended All Saints' Church with his master's family. But when he was passing down College Lane one Sunday he was attracted by the singing in the Baptist chapel, went in, and was converted. He was baptized in the River Nene by Dr. Ryland in 1798, and soon began to do some village preaching. On a visit home his mother said to him: "John, they tell me thee hast become a meetinger. . . . Tell me all about it"; and John told her to such effect that she came to share his faith. In 1805 John Wheeler set up for himself as a tallow-chandler in the village of Bugbrooke, where he and five others from College Lane were formed into a Baptist Church, to which he became the minister for more than thirty years. Thomas Wheeler, his brother, " thought he was religious enough " until he also came to Northampton on the advice of John, and there came under the same influences, but he was not baptized until he was at Dunstable. Here he heard Robert Hall preach, and was so deeply impressed that the next morning he gave his master notice to leave, saying that he must sit under such a ministry. He followed Robert Hall to Leicester, told him what he had done, and asked for help in finding a situation there. Robert Hall is reported to have drawn himself up to his full height and to have said: " I never was so complimented in my life, sir. I will go with you at once, sir, and see if I can find you a situation "—which he did. Thomas became a deacon eventually at the Harvey Lane Church. Meanwhile a third son, Francis, had followed his brothers to Northampton, and was baptized by the College Lane minister in 1812. The Church sent him to the Bristol Baptist College to be trained for the ministry, and he eventually became minister of the Moulton Baptist Church (where Carey had been the minister) and remained there for over thirty years. Whilst Francis was an apprentice, he was the means of the conversion of a fellow-apprentice who in later life is said to have turned the mind of Park Street Church to the young man called Charles Haddon Spurgeon. One of the converts of John Wheeler at Bugbrooke was John Turland Brown, the future minister of College Street, Northampton, and a future President of the Baptist Union. An apprentice, Hail Marriott Mawby, who married his master's daughter, rendered devoted service as a deacon and Sunday-school worker at Long Buckby and at College Street, Northampton.[1]

This homely narrative owes its value to its homeliness, for it is typical of the propagation of the Baptist faith in what we may call the middle period of its history. There was, however, some corporate as well as individual realization of mis-

---

[1] The account is taken from an unpublished manuscript by the late Benjamin Wheeler, son of Francis Wheeler, written in 1881, of which a copy is in my possession, made by H. M. Mawby. To the latter, as it is only right to acknowledge in such a connection, I owe all my opportunities for education.

sionary duty, even as when the Church at Antioch sent out Barnabas and Paul as its missionary representatives. Dr. Whitley, writing of the Baptist Churches in the seventeenth century, says: "The first distinctive feature was the recognition of the duty of evangelization and telling off special men for itinerant work.[1] . . . At first there was a separate commission for each journey; soon they selected men who had peculiar aptitude for evangelization, told them off for it as their main work, and undertook to support them and their families. . . . Thus the Messenger came to be a regular officer, not of one Church, but of a group of Churches; every such group came to realize its duty to support a missionary, every new Church was trained to realize its duty in this respect. This development went on in both groups of Baptists" (i.e. the Generals and the Particulars).[2]

In the eighteenth century the Baptist Churches shared in the general decline of religious fervour which preceded the Evangelical Revival. The "soft shell" of Arminianism was not a sufficient protection of the General Baptists against doctrinal decay, and (apart from the "New Connexion" of 1770) they cease to count. The "hard shell" of Calvinism protected the Particular Baptists from disintegration, but brought its own perils, which have been partly illustrated in the study of Ann Dutton (pp. 50 ff.). It would not be fair to make either the lack of the missionary spirit or moral "antinomianism" the necessary consequence of the Calvinistic doctrine of predestination, for Whitefield's Calvinism was joined to Wesley's Arminianism in the Evangelical Revival, and Arminianism as well as Calvinism has had to rebuke those who neglected the moral law on the ground of religious faith. But the experience of Andrew Fuller (1754-1815) as a young pastor will show how "hyper-Calvinism" could be made to

---

[1] The Fenstanton *Records*, pp. 72 ff. describe such a preaching tour by Henry Denne, duly appointed a Messenger by the Fenstanton Church.

[2] *History of British Baptists*, pp. 87, 88. Of the fifteen men who signed the Particular Baptist Confession of 1644, "every one who can be traced was an ardent evangelist" (p. 89). Cf. the resolution of the Kentish Association (1657): "Agreed that there be all possible care in propagateing the Gospel by Imploying the Messengers in the work of the Lord Jesus sending with each of them one young disciple . . . also that theire ffamilies be well provided for in their absence" (*op. cit.*, p. 68).

justify the lack of missionary zeal. He had been brought up in what he calls the "shackles" of such a distinction between the "elect" and the "reprobate" that the duty as well as the possibility of saving faith was confined to the former. It is evident that such a distinction so applied would inevitably fetter the preacher in his appeals to the unconverted for whom nothing but the duty of obedience to the external law was obligatory. But by 1781 young Fuller had discovered that such a distinction was made neither by the Bible nor by such men as Eliott [1] and Brainerd in their preaching to American Indians. Fuller therefore worked out his freedom to preach to all the duty of faith, and the promise of forgiveness to every penitent sinner, without any abandonment of the doctrines of Calvinism proper (it was common ground that *saving* faith, could be experienced only by the elect). In 1785 he published his results in a book entitled *The Gospel of Christ worthy of all acceptation, or the obligations of men fully to credit and cordially to approve whatever God makes known*. This book had important consequences, not only for Baptists, but also for the world. "Fullerism", as it was called, created a considerable controversy, but it offered an open door to those who were feeling the breath of the Evangelical Revival. Amongst these was a young Baptist minister who had to earn part of his living by keeping school and making shoes. William Carey (1761-1834) was in close personal touch with Andrew Fuller, of Kettering, and saw the application of his truth to a wider field of duty. At Moulton he had read Captain Cook's *Journal*, and had been kindled to missionary enthusiasm by its revelation of human need. At a ministers' meeting in 1786 he first raised the question "whether the command given to the Apostles to teach all nations was not obligatory on all succeeding ministers to the end of the world, seeing that the accompanying promise was of equal extent"; but he was told by John Collett Ryland to sit down: "You're an enthusiast. When God pleases to convert the heathen, He'll do it without consulting you or me."[2] But in 1792 William Carey, then at Leicester, brought out a book of 87 pages, entitled, *An Enquiry into the Obligations of Christians, to use*

---

[1] Weitbrecht speaks of his work as "the first real Protestant missionary enterprise" (*Encyclopædia of Religion and Ethics*, viii, p. 729).
[2] *William Carey*, by S. Pearce Carey, 8th ed., p. 54.

means for the conversion of the heathens, in which the religious state of the different nations of the world, the success of former undertakings, and the practicability of further undertakings, are considered.[1] It is a great book, both in itself, in relation to its author, and in its historical issues. Already we may see in its plain and scientific marshalling of facts, its absence of rhetoric, its cogent insistence on a proved duty, those qualities of mind and character which made Carey the great man he was. He first asks the question he had raised in 1786 and had been persistently raising ever since—" whether the commission given by our Lord to His disciples be not still binding on us ". He reviews the history of missions through the centuries in a way that shows his wide knowledge and reading. He patiently tabulates the countries of the world, their populations and their religions, according to contemporary knowledge. He faces the practical difficulties in the way of foreign missionary work, and disposes of them one by one. Finally, he sets out the example and methods of a trading company which has obtained a charter, and proposes the formation of a missionary society on the same lines to undertake the practical work of evangelization abroad. " We have only to keep the end in view, and have our hearts thoroughly engaged in the pursuit of it, and means will not be very difficult."

His proposal was carried into effect in the autumn of 1792 at Kettering, after it had been enforced at Nottingham in the spring by Carey's well-known sermon, " Expect great things from God ; attempt great things for God ", and the new chartered company started with a subscribed capital of £13 2s. 6d. Its first operation was to send out William Carey to Bengal as colleague to John Thomas, a Baptist doctor who had already done some missionary work there.[2] Carey's intensely practical mind and general efficiency enabled him not only to become self-supporting, but to earn large sums of money

[1] See photographic reproduction, Carey Press, 1934.
[2] Mr. F. D. Walker's discriminating study, *William Carey*, shows his true place in the history of Protestant foreign missions. "He was not the 'Father of modern Missions'; he was not 'the first Englishman to go out as a missionary to the heathen'; he was not 'the first missionary to India'. He was the founder of the Baptist Missionary Society ; he was one of the first two Englishmen sent by a Missionary Society as missionaries to the non-Christians of India" (p. 103). The faults of John Thomas have helped to hide his primacy. "He was

which were unselfishly devoted to missionary work. His great powers as a linguist had already been shown in the acquisition of half a dozen languages whilst at home. In India he eventually became Professor of Sanscrit at Fort William College, and achieved an amazing amount of translation work in the missionary interest through his indefatigable industry and undaunted courage. His chief helpers were Joshua Marshman, first a weaver, then a schoolmaster, and from 1799 at work with Carey in Serampore, and William Ward, a printer and newspaper editor, whom the far-sighted Carey had earmarked before his departure from England. " The distinguishing characteristic of Carey's work was his adoption of the principle of concentration. It is true that he sent agents to distribute his translations of the Bible and to attempt to found mission-stations in places far distant from Serampore, but his life-work was the establishment of the training college at Serampore and of the group of schools in its neighbourhood. To a far greater extent than any of his predecessors he realized the comparative futility of diffused missions and the impossibility of converting India by means of European evangelists." [1] The Baptist Missionary Society is at present working in Bengal, Bihar and Orissa,[2] and North India, as well as in Ceylon (from 1812), the educational emphasis being specially prominent in its Indian work.

The missionary passion of the Society, sustained and led at home by the loyal devotion and remarkable energies of Andrew Fuller, sought an outlet in the West as well as in the East, and work in Jamaica was taken up in 1814, and for a considerable time received almost as much attention and support as that in India. Its outstanding feature of interest was the part taken by William Knibb (1803-45) in the abolition

the first Englishman set apart for definite missionary work in India, and the first to lead an Indian to the Saviour " (*op. cit.*, p. 228). There is a *Life* of him by C. B. Lewis (1873). But all this does not materially affect the universal recognition of Carey as the great pioneer in modern foreign missionary work. See K. S. Latourette, *A History of the Expansion of Christianity*, iv. p. 68: "He was the first Anglo-Saxon Protestant either in America or in Great Britain to propose that Christians take concrete steps to bring their Gospel to all the human race."

[1] *History of Christian Missions*, by C. H. Robinson, pp. 82, 83.

[2] The work in Orissa was carried on by the General Baptists from 1816 till 1891.

of slavery, to which reference will be made in the next chapter. The Jamaican Baptist Churches, counting over 30,000 members, were long self-supporting, though Calabar College was sustained from Britain.[1] Another field of the Society's work was the Cameroons, on the West Coast of Africa (opposite to the island of Fernando Po, the scene of its first attempt), where flourished still the slave-trade that had so largely populated Jamaica. "Soon after gaining his freedom, a man named Keith worked his passage from Jamaica, and proclaimed the Gospel on the very spot where he had been made a slave."[2] The first Baptist mission-station on the continent of Africa was established in 1845 by Alfred Saker, who came to be known as "the Apostle of the Cameroons". It is significant that the first real impression on the Dualla natives was made by Saker's brickyard, for bricks could resist white ants.[3] The African missionary has usually had to be ready to turn his hand to any and every occupation. On the transference of the Cameroons to Germany in 1884 the Baptist work was handed over to German missionaries, but before this a new opening for African work was found on the newly discovered Congo River (of which the mouth is about as far south of the equator as the Cameroons are north of it). In 1878 George Grenfell and Thomas Comber, who had been working with Saker, came to San Salvador, and began the most picturesque and romantic as well as the most arduous work of the Society. It was inevitable that the pioneer missionary should be, like Livingstone, an explorer, and here George Grenfell won high distinction, fully recognized in the two fine volumes devoted to his work by Sir Harry Johnston. With Grenfell's name is linked that of Holman Bentley,[4] who was the pioneer in linguistic work on Congo languages and dialects, of which

---

[1] See E. A. Payne, *Freedom in Jamaica*, 1933. (It seems likely that in the years ahead renewed help from the Baptist Missionary Society may be desirable. Work has also been done with permanent results elsewhere in the West Indies, e.g. Trinidad.)

[2] *The Centenary Volume of the B.M.S.*, p. 16.

[3] Sir Harry Johnston, *George Grenfell and the Congo*, vol. i, p. 35; see also *The Life of George Grenfell*, by George Hawker (1909).

[4] *W. Holman Bentley*, by H. M. Bentley (1907); see also his own *Pioneering on the Congo*, 1900. Vol. i, pp. 57 ff., refers to the generosity of Robert Arthington, of Leeds, in this connection. He left a large bequest, used for expansion on many fields.

there are said to be two hundred. The most fully developed part of the mission is in the Congo language area, in the cataract stretch of the river between Matadi and Stanley Pool, but the stations of the Society extend over a thousand miles of the Congo River as far as Yakusu.[1] There is, moreover, extensive American Baptist missionary work in the Congo territory.

It is needless to say that in this new land the cost in human lives has been very heavy, from the time of the Combers onwards. But the greater physical peril and hardship bring a relatively greater visible return. It is a native Congo belief that the stars are the watch-fires of villages in the sky, for, as their primitive logic says, " the rain puts them out." In sober truth, the scattered stations of missionary work in the " Dark Continent " are centres of light and warmth, which none of the elemental forces will be able to extinguish.

The third great area of Baptist missionary work is in the provinces of Shantung, Shansi and Shensi, in Northern China, right, left and right of the great Yellow River, which, unlike the dense population of its shores, has cut so many new beds for itself in the course of the centuries.[2] Serious work began in 1870 with the arrival of Timothy Richard in Shantung, and his name remains the outstanding one in this field. He was prominent in the work of relief in the great famine of 1876-78, which was the occasion of the extension of missionary work from Shantung to the inland Shansi. Of this and other activities, including influential relations with high officials, a characteristically detailed account is given in Dr. Richard's valuable book, *Forty-Five Years in China*.[3] He laid special stress on the importance of Christian literature for missionary work in China, and was prominent in the work of the Christian Literature Society after 1891. He became Chancellor of the Shansi·University, which was founded by the Chinese Government in 1901 out of the fine levied upon the province because of the Boxer outrages. There is also a

[1] See *Achievement*, by F. Townley Lord, 1942, an interesting popular account of the whole work of the Baptist Missionary Society, prepared for the ter-jubilee. Missionary work was done in Italy from 1870 and in Brittany from 1843.

[2] Meredith Townsend, *Asia and Europe*, p. 279. This appears to have been the original seat of the Chinese, no immigration being indicated (Moore, *History of Religions*, i, p. 1).

[3] There is a biography of him by W. E. Soothill (1923).

Christian University of Shantung, in which Baptists have an important share ; as in India, the educational side of evangelistic work receives increasing attention, together with a full recognition of the value of medical missions. The Boxer massacres of Shansi missionaries and Chinese Christians in 1900, springing from an intense anti-foreign propaganda, wrote a tragic page in the history of Baptist missions as well as of those of other Churches. At Tai-yuan-fu, where a company of forty-six missionaries or their children were massacred, a considerable proportion were Baptists, and eight represented the Baptist Missionary Society ; from Sinchow another company of eight escaped into hiding in caves of the hills, only to be run down at last and massacred. The story of their sufferings [1] is like the acts of the martyrs in the early history of the Church, and, like all earnest missionary life, these common deaths preach the catholicity of truth, deeper than all denominational differences of judgment and conviction.

The missionary spirit is, of course, not the characteristic of any branch of the universal Church, but is found wherever there is vigorous Christian life and personal loyalty to the Head of the Church. But it may fairly be claimed that the *emphasis* on the missionary duty and the response to that emphasis displayed since Carey's day do characterize Baptist Church life. Its keenest interests and its chief form of corporate activity are found here. Indeed, what the " Church " is to some other communions, the " Missionary Society " is to many Baptists. As someone once remarked to the present writer, " It is in the missionary meeting that you may hear the beating of the Baptist heart ". The work done on the foreign field since Carey's time will compare by no means unfavourably with that of other Churches, with greater resources of men and money, so far as Great Britain is concerned. As we review it, even in so rapid an outline as that just given, certain features become apparent, significant for Baptists, as indeed for all Christians.

There is increasing recognition—indeed, general recognition to-day—that the future of missionary work must lie with native evangelists and the growth of native Churches. This is not merely an inference from the magnitude of the work to

[1] See *The China Martyrs of* 1900, by R. C. Forsyth (1904).

be done; it is discernment of the best way of doing it. Dr. Richard[1] remarks on the bringing in of fifty inquirers by one Chinese Bible-woman and of one hundred by another: "This proved for the hundredth time the fact that natives can best influence their fellow-countrymen to join the Christian Church". The recognition of this fact will not mean a lightening of the missionary responsibility of the Church, for the training and oversight of these native leaders will need all the devotion of men and money the Church can bring; but it will mean that the Christian faith will be interpreted by the native mind to the native mind, and that some of the results may not be those which would entirely agree with our Western interpretation. This line of thought has been forcibly presented most recently by Mr. Stanley Jones in his widely-read book, *The Christ of the Indian Road*, which is a plea for native liberty of interpretation, joined with a healthy confidence in the ultimate result. There should be less hesitation amongst Baptists as to this liberty than amongst those who are committed to a formal creed. The liberty that Baptists have claimed and won for themselves they must be prepared to give to others.

A further principle of modern missionary work is that it must erase some of the old lines drawn between "sacred" and "secular" activity, and be prepared to expand into all forms of usefulness that promote the extension of the Kingdom of God. This principle has not been easily reached, and we can see what it cost some of the greatest missionaries to convince those who were not face to face with the facts, like themselves. Even now many good people who support "missions" would be startled to realize that a missionary is not "preaching" the Gospel all the time, and that many things have to be done before it can be preached at all. But all these things belong to the Kingdom of God, if they do not belong to the Church as its nucleus and centre. When in 1801 Carey, Marshman, and Ward laid on the Communion Table the first Bengali New Testament—the result of seven and a half years of labour[2] they were consecrating Christian scholarship in the widest sense, and implicitly opening the door to all that educational work which Carey so valued, just as the baptism of the first Indian convert, Krishna Pal, was

[1] *Forty-Five Years in China*, p. 216.
[2] *William Carey*, by S. P. Carey, 8th ed., p. 211.

the consecration of the medical skill that had set his dislocated shoulder and won his loyalty to the Saviour John Thomas preached. No modern missionary has had a wider horizon in this respect than Dr. Timothy Richàrd, and we have seen that his work in famine relief opened up a new province to Baptist missions. The exploration of the Congo by Grenfell and Bentley was just as truly the work of the Gospel as the foundation of stations on its banks which their work made possible. All this is generally granted to-day, for it is in the line of our modern humanitarian emphasis. But Christians in general have not yet seen all the consequences of this new vision of the Christianization of all things by the purpose and the spirit in which they are done.

This leads directly to the question of the missionary motive. An illuminating summary by Canon Quick may be quoted: " Sometimes the motive has been the desire to save something more out of a wreck doomed to destruction by the forces of evil which are overwhelming it. Sometimes it has been the desire to herald and advance the reign of Christ upon the earth itself. Other-worldly Christianity has been inspired by the first motive, evolutionary Christianity by the second. Possibly the noblest motive of all is the passion to share and to serve the creative purpose of God, to make something on earth and out of earth, which is fit to be the eternal object of God's love ".[1]

This broader outlook, though it implies much greater sympathy with the large elements of truth in many non-Christian faiths, does not necessarily mean the perilous compromise with heathen customs. Baptist missionaries are often face to face with the same issue as the earliest preachers of the faith—how far is it expedient to baptize heathen customs as well as heathen converts? How far, for example, can the initiation rites of many tribes be permitted to continue in some modified form? How far is caste to be recognized? In general, it may be said that the Baptist missionaries have been unequivocal in demanding a clear cut from those practices that are bound up with superstition, and a clear sacrifice of the old standing and attitude in the name of the new faith. The value of believers' baptism by immersion is evident in this respect. Baptists seek genuine conversion and not merely

---

[1] *Catholic and Protestant Elements of Christianity*, p. 102.

a general uplift, and they recognize the peril of "Mass Movements". Their success has been marked amongst people of the sturdy, independent type, e.g. the Lushais.

When the Baptist Missionary Society began its work abroad in 1793, it was inevitable that it should be met with the criticism which, like economic poverty, we have always with us—that there were plenty of heathen at home.[1] They met this by undertaking itinerant preaching at home, and there was, for example, in 1796, a lengthy evangelistic tour by two appointed ministers in Cornwall. One of the two was William Steadman, who afterwards became the first President of the Northern Education Society (now Rawdon College), and made itinerancy a marked feature of the work of himself and his students. In 1797, however, a society to promote home evangelism was formed in London, and carried on a work that became very extensive at certain periods, a hundred whole-time agents being employed in 1835.[2] In 1879, however, the work of the Home Mission was taken over by the Baptist Union, which continued the previous development of policy in the direction of founding or supporting mission churches rather than itinerancy. Home mission work of this kind is now done rather through the Associations, with their more intimate knowledge of local conditions. Considerable progress has also been made in the organization of lay preachers.

No attempt can here be made to speak of the missionary spirit amongst American Baptists, from the time when Roger Williams, the first American Baptist, worked amongst the Indians (c. 1630) to the present day of the great American Baptist Societies for both home and foreign missionary work, which are proportionate to the magnitude of a leading denomination.[3] It is the less necessary to do so because we are not concerned with making a catalogue or writing a history, but with the missionary spirit of the denomination, which is illustrated as well in the smaller group in Great Britain as in the much larger group in the United States.

[1] Whitley, op. cit., p. 266.
[2] *The Story of Baptist Home Missions*, by C. Brown, p. 32 (1897).
[3] "It is significant that the call to engage in foreign mission work was the first thing that led to organization and unity among Baptists in the country" of America (*Directory* of the Baptist World Alliance, 1927, p. 46). This was in 1814.

The fact is that the Christian faith is imperialistic; it cannot be content to be accepted as a useful institution, a beautiful if impracticable dream, one among many guesses at truth, or even as one religious truth amongst others. There is a noble as well as an ignoble intolerance—an intolerance of compromise which claims an imperial dominion with imperial confidence for an imperial truth, in the spirit in which the greatest missionary is seen standing in Rome uttering his last recorded message : "This salvation of God is sent unto the nations ; they will also hear."[1]

[1] Acts xxviii. 28.

VI

THE PASSION OF THE BAPTISTS FOR LIBERTY

IN the first paragraph of Milton's *Areopagitica*, that typically English defence of liberty, he speaks of the "passion" engendered by his subject and the occasion, the order of the Puritan Parliament forbidding the publication of any unlicensed book.[1] The passion of the Baptists for liberty is one of their most strongly marked characteristics, flowing directly from the spiritual individualism which is their primary emphasis. From the beginning of their history Baptists have been in the forefront of the battle for political and religious liberty, as their place in Cromwell's army shows. To them belongs the distinction of being the first to claim and the first to apply fearlessly the unfettered principle of freedom for religion,[2] which is the best tribute to its intrinsic worth. Their phenomenal growth in the United States of America must be partly due to this characteristic passion, so congenial to a constitution framed on the basis of political and religious equality and freedom.

---

[1] Milton held Baptist views, though of unorthodox variety. Cf. *A Treatise on Christian Doctrine*, p. 431 (ed. 1825): "Baptism, wherein the bodies of believers who engage themselves to pureness of life are immersed in running water, to signify their regeneration by the Holy Spirit, and their union with Christ in His death, burial and resurrection" (in the Latin ed., p. 317). On the other hand, his peculiar Christology (Arian rather than Socinian) separates him from Baptists in general, with whom he does not seem to have been in corporate communion. See Whitley, *A History of British Baptists*, Note C: "In what sense was Milton a Baptist?"

[2] Cf. W. F. Adeney (himself a Congregationalist) in the *Encyclopædia of Religion and Ethics*, ix. p. 382: "It should be observed that, while modern Nonconformists are opposed to any interference with religion by the State, and stand for complete religious liberty—Cavour's 'free Church in a free State'—this was by no means the case among the early Nonconformists, with the solitary exception of the Baptists." So also Skeats and Miall, *History of the Free Churches of England*, p. 19.

Already in John Smyth, the first Baptist, we find the explicit claim for full religious freedom:—

That the magistrate is not by vertue of his office to meddle with religion, or matters of conscience, to force and compell men to this or that form of religion, or doctrine: but to leaue Christian religion free, to euery mans conscience, and to handle onely ciuil transgressions Rom. 13. injuries and wronges of men against man, in murther, Adulterie, theft, etc. for Christ onelie is the king, and lawgiver of the church and conscience Jas 4. 12.—(*A Confession of Faith*, 1611, art. 84.)

But the first publication of such a claim is found in the black-letter 16mo called *A short declaration of the Mistery of Iniquity*, by Thomas Helwys, a foremost disciple of Smyth's.[1] In 1612 he felt it his duty to leave his master in Amsterdam and return to England, in order to testify openly to his Baptist faith. He had thus won the right to challenge his fellow-Separatists in Holland to "come and lay down their lives in their owne Countrie for Christ and His truth."[2] Thomas Helwys knew the risks he ran in publishing under his own name so direct an attack on authority as this. "Let none thinke that we are altogether ignorant, what building and what war fare we take in hand, and that we have not sitt downe and in some measure thoroughly considered what the cost and danger may be". He was soon in prison and lost to our sight. The doctrine of full religious liberty, now so much a commonplace, then so perilous and fanatical an innovation, is definite and reiterated in this book, e.g.:—

Our lord the King is but an earthly King, and he hath no aucthority as a King but in earthly causes, and if the Kings people be obedient and true subjects, obeying all humane lawes made by the King, our lord the King can require no more: for mens religion to God is betwixt God and themselves; the King shall not answere for it, neither may the King be iugd betwene God and man. Let them be heretikes, Turcks, Jewes or whatsoever, it apperteynes not to the earthly power to punish them in the least measure (p. 69).

This book has historic importance, as being the first published English assertion of this doctrine.[3] It was soon

[1] See the reproduction by Replika process issued by the Baptist Historical Society in 1935.
[2] *Op. cit.*, p. 112.
[3] So Whitley, *op. cit.*, p. 33.

followed by similar testimony from fellow-Baptists, such as Leonard Busher in *Religion's Peace* (1614) and John Murton in *Objections Answered* (1615) and *An Humble Supplication* (1620).[1] This last had a romantic origin and a historic issue, both deserving to be remembered. Of its origin we are told by Roger Williams, who in 1644 incorporated some of its argument in his book, *The Bloudy Tenent of Persecution*: —

> The author of these arguments against persecution, as I have been informed, being committed by some then in power close prisoner to Newgate, for the witness of some truths of Jesus, and having not the use of pen and ink, wrote these arguments in milk, in sheets of paper brought to him by the woman, his keeper, from a friend in London as the stopples of his milk bottle. In such paper written with milk, nothing will appear ; but the way of reading it by fire being known to this friend who received the papers, he transcribed and kept together the papers, although the author himself could not correct, nor view what himself had written (*op. cit.*, p. 36 of 1848 ed.).

Roger Williams, who had emigrated to America in 1630, found as much intolerance of unorthodox opinions amongst the Puritans of New England as amongst the Anglicans of the old England, even though it was less violently expressed. He was banished from Massachusetts in 1635, and in the following year founded the settlement of Rhode Island, which had the distinction of being the first to grant full religious liberty. Roger Williams became a Baptist in 1639, and founded the first Baptist Church in America. His pioneer work in both civil rights and religious propaganda thus links itself with the book written in Newgate prison on the stopples of bottles in the milk they contained, and is inseparably interwoven with the world's history. " In subjection, in exile, in power, Baptists preached and practised religious liberty ; and from little Rhode Island the principle has been adopted as fundamental in the whole United States of America."[2]

The legal position of the first English Baptists was defined by the Elizabethan Act of 1593 directed against " seditious

---

[1] All these are given in the first volume published by the Hanserd Knollys Society, *Tracts on Liberty of Conscience* (1846). Copies of the very rare book by Helwys are to be found in the Bodleian, Trinity College, Dublin, and in the Angus Library, Regent's Park College. For the significance of Helwys and Murton see Burgess, *John Smith, etc.*, 1911.

[2] Whitley, *op. cit.*, p. 67.

sectaries and disloyal persons ".[1] Absence from the established worship for one month or presence at a " conventicle " caused liability to imprisonment; non-submission within three months involved banishment from the realm. John Smyth and the other Puritan Separatists of Gainsborough and Scrooby were therefore simply anticipating the law when they voluntarily withdrew from England to Holland; indeed, some of them did not escape imprisonment.[2] When Thomas Helwys and his friends returned to London in 1612 the old law was still in operation, but they could now also be required to take the oath of allegiance, originally (in 1606) extracted from " Popish Recusants ". They had, of course, no personal difficulty in this, but the ecclesiastical authorities wished to debar them from its protection, as it was not intended to cover the case of Separatists.[3] Thus we find a Baptist petition of 1614, probably from Helwys and his friends in prison, which points out the injustice of this discrimination: " When wee fall under the handes of the Bishops wee can have no benefitt by the said oath, for they say it belongeth onely to Popish recuzantes, and not to others."[4] The civil power was more reasonable. It is worthy of notice that these petitioners expressly refuse the calumniating identification of themselves with the " Anabaptists ".

In spite of these legal disabilities and penalties, Baptist Churches contrived to maintain their corporate existence, even when the advent of Laud (Bishop of London, 1628; Archbishop of Canterbury, 1633) brought with it a more vigorous policy of persecution. For the period prior to 1640, when the assembling of the "Long" Parliament began a new era, we hear of six Baptist groups, two in London, the other four at Lincoln, Salisbury, Coventry, and Tiverton.[5] These were all of the " General " (i.e. Arminian) type. There is no

[1] Gee and Hardy, *Documents illustrative of the History of the English Church*, lxxxvi.
[2] Burgess, *op. cit.*, p. 94.
[3] Whitley, *op. cit.*, p. 38. He gives a clear summary of the two distinct sets of officials concerned in the administration of the law—the civil (sheriffs, magistrates, county judges, Star Chamber) and the ecclesiastical (archdeacons, bishops, archbishops, High Commission). See also Frere, *A History of the English Church in the Reigns of Elizabeth and James I*, pp. 350 ff.
[4] Burrage, *The Early English Dissenters*, ii, p. 215, where the whole petition is printed.
[5] Particulars will be found in Whitley, *op. cit.*, pp. 45-58.

evidence of any Churches of the other type (the "Particular", i.e. Calvinistic) until the closing years of the period, though this (not without important modification) was destined to form the Baptist Church of the future. The subterranean continuance of Baptist life between 1620 and 1640 is shown by the gathered force of the current when the stream breaks into the open, and the rise of Puritanism into power gave Baptists their opportunity. It is an interesting coincidence that Oliver Cromwell first came into military prominence at Gainsborough in 1643, when he was successful in relieving the town, besieged by the Royalists.[1] Thus the place which saw John Smyth begin to express those convictions which issued in his becoming the first Baptist also saw the first notable victory of the Puritan leader, who was to draw so much of his military strength from Baptist ranks. We owe it to Dr. Whitley that the place of Baptists in Cromwell's army has been brought to light in its full extent.[2] The use of the term "Independent" to designate the religious texture of the army as distinct from the "Presbyterian" Parliament (1640-48) has obscured the fact that " the New Model Army " was largely recruited and officered from Baptists. A typical example has been given in the study of William Allen, adjutant-general (see Chapter II, §2). Other well-known names include those of Richard Deane, artillery general and subsequently admiral, associated with Blake and buried in Westminster Abbey ; Thomas Harrison, prominent throughout the whole period, who held chief command in Cromwell's absence (1650-51), impressive by his unshaken conviction and courage when executed in 1660 ; Colonel Hutchinson, a Baptist of different mould, who escaped the penalty of regicide by submission, and has been made familiar to us by his wife's memoirs and by J. R. Green's illustrative use of him as a cultured Puritan ; Edmund Ludlow, prominent in connection with "Pride's Purge" in 1648, Commander-in-Chief in Ireland, 1659, who wrote his own memoirs in exile (twenty-five of his regimental officers were members of Baptist churches); Robert Lilburne, Commander-in-Chief in Scotland in 1654, and brother of John Lilburne, the Leveller leader, who also as a young man seems to have had Baptist contacts ;

[1] Carlyle, *Oliver Cromwell*, i, p. 138.
[2] *Op. cit.*, pp. 73-81.

William Gough, one of Cromwell's "Lords" and one of the four who were sent by the army to meet Monck.[1]

The place taken by these men and many others who could be named shows the passion of the Baptists for that religious liberty which had been so unjustly denied to them. Their political motives were distinctly subordinate to religious aims, as was true of Puritanism in general.[2] But it is seen more clearly in the Baptists than in others, because of their general opposition to Cromwell's political policy after the execution of Charles. This has been illustrated in the case of William Allen; it could be illustrated also from most of those named above. They would not have "a ghost from the grave" of the Stuarts to tyrannize over them. The extreme form of this opposition was found in the "Fifth-Monarchy" movement, in which many Baptists were implicated.[3] The movement drew its name from "the kingdom of the saints" pictured in Daniel vii. as arising after the rule of the four beasts. They illustrated one of the many types of contemporary religious fanaticism. The movement culminated and collapsed in the armed rising of Thomas Venner in 1661, which naturally helped to discredit the Baptists, and drew from them many disavowals of it.[4]

The general position of the Baptists from 1640 to 1660 was naturally one of greater religious freedom, though with considerable variety of expression as the political movements of that kaleidoscopic time affected them. In the army, as we have just seen, and naturally where the army had control, they were protected—at least as soon as the army came into Cromwell's hands. He stood up for them and for others like

---

[1] Brief accounts of all these men will be found in the *Dictionary of National Biography*. There is an edition of the very interesting *Memoirs of Colonel Hutchinson*, with notes by C. H. Firth (1906). Ludlow's *Memoirs*, in three volumes, were first published in 1698-99; they are frequently cited by Carlyle, with the adjectives "solid" or "wooden" Ludlow. The well-known description of the ejection of the "Rump" will be found in ii, pp. 455 f.; he derived it from Harrison.

[2] Trevelyan, *History of England*, pp. 375, 381. Cf. his remark on Laud's ecclesiastical policy: "It was indeed the chief cause of the Civil War, because it provoked the furious reaction of armed Puritanism in which Laud himself perished" (p. 393).

[3] See *Baptists and Fifth-Monarchy Men*, by L. F. Brown (1912). We may compare the relation of the Zealots to Pharisaism in the New Testament period.

[4] Whitley, *op. cit.*, p. 109.

them against the Presbyterian Puritans, who were as intolerant as Anglicans had been. "Honest men served you faithfully in this action. Sir, they are trusty; I beseech you, in the name of God, not to discourage them. . . . He that ventures his life for the liberty of his country, I wish he trust God for the liberty of his conscience, and you for the liberty he fights for."[1] Cromwell in his Protectorate gave expression to his ideas of comprehension and toleration. "While he preserved tithe and endowments, he put down persecution. The benefices of the Church were held by Presbyterians, Independents, or Baptists indifferently, while free congregations of a more fanciful kind multiplied outside. . . . The fatal flaw in his ecclesiastical policy was that he had not been able to give Anglicanism that share in the life of the Church which he had offered to grant it in the Heads of the Proposals."[2]

In the reaction from Puritan intolerance and political incapacity which characterized the Restoration of 1660, Baptists inevitably entered upon a period of severe persecution, lasting with intervals until the final settlement of the Revolution in 1689. They were not greatly concerned with the Act of Uniformity of 1662, which completed the expulsion of some 2,000 "Nonconformist" clergymen from the Established Church. Indeed, this expulsion indirectly benefited them, for it reinforced dissent with a number of able and cultured men, which it greatly needed. But the revengeful spirit of the "Cavalier Parliament", which began in 1661 its seventeen-year-long tenure of power, found expression in the successive enactments of the so-called "Clarendon Code". In its first year the Corporation Act required magistrates and other municipal officers to have "taken the Sacrament of the Lord's Supper, according to the rites of the Church of England"

---

[1] Letter of June 14, 1645; quoted in Carlyle's *Cromwell*, i, p. 192. How little the warning was heeded is seen in the fact that "the Long Parliament, with almost incredible folly, proceeded to pass measures for the lifelong imprisonment of Baptists, the prohibition of laymen from preaching in public, and the dismissal of all Independent officers from the New Model" (Trevelyan, *op. cit.*, p. 418).

[2] Trevelyan, *op. cit.*, pp. 430,431. The actual number of Baptists in the Established Church of this period was smaller than has been supposed. Whitley calculates that in 1659-60 "there were not more than thirty Baptists who were drawing public money for religious work; of these about a dozen may have been clergy" (p. 160).

within the year previous to their election.[1] This exclusion of Dissenters from municipal office affected only a small number of Baptists, but its moral and indirect effect was far-reaching. In 1664, however, they came under the ban of a temporary Conventicle Act,[2] which inflicted heavy fines or imprisonment, or ultimate transportation or death, on any person over sixteen attending "any assembly, conventicle or meeting, under colour or pretence of any exercise of religion, in other manner than according to the liturgy and practice of the Church of England", if there were five present beyond those of the same household. Prior to the passing of the Act, Baptists were already suffering (from 1660) under the revival of the old Elizabethan Act of Uniformity and Conventicle Act, though the Star Chamber and High Commission Court were not revived; it was under the Elizabethan Conventicle Act that the imprisonment of John Bunyan began in 1660, continuing until 1672. The fortunes of a Baptist Church from 1660 onwards can be followed in the story of the Broadmead Church of Bristol.[3] As an example of the expedients to which they were driven, a paragraph of 1670 may be quoted:—

because we did not know which way they would begin upon us, we shut our public meeting-house door when we understood they were coming. Then they (the informers) fetched constables, and broke open the door, came in, and took our names, for which some of us were brought before the magistrates and convicted. Then, against the next Lord's day, we broke a wall, up on high, for a window, and put the speaker in the next house to stand and preach, whereby we heard him as well as if in the room with us. The bishop's informers come in again, take our names, for which we were again brought before the mayor, and convicted. So they did the third Lord's day. And the fourth Lord's day, the mayor himself, with his officers and some aldermen, came upon us, and turned us out; but seeing they could not make us refrain our meeting, they raised the train bands every last day of the week, in the evening, one band to keep us out of our places, and nailed up our doors, and put locks upon them; so they kept

---

[1] Gee and Hardy, *op. cit.*, cxvi.
[2] *Ibid.*, cxix, for the permanent Conventicle Act of 1670, which inflicted fines only, and operated till 1813. Public opinion would not tolerate the severity of the earlier form of the Act.
[3] *The Records of a Church of Christ Meeting in Broadmead, Bristol,* 1640-1687 (Hanserd Knollys Society, 1847).

us out by force and power, that we were fain to meet in the lanes and highways for several months (pp. 105, 106).

In 1665 the Five Mile Act was passed, directed against the Nonconformist clergy and other preachers, who had held official livings (of whom there were about thirty Baptists), requiring an oath of acceptance of the *status quo*, failing which such persons were forbidden to reside within five miles of the place of their ministry or to keep any school.[1] This was the last Act of the "Clarendon Code" proper, but in 1673 the Test Act was added, which extended the provisions of the Corporation Act by excluding consistent Nonconformists from all Government employment.[2]

In 1672 the unconstitutional claim of Charles to exercise dispensing power by a Declaration of Indulgence (which he had to withdraw) benefited some Baptists, including Bunyan. In 1687 James tried the same device in the interests of Roman Catholicism, but few Baptists welcomed it, for it was clear to most of them that relief would be purchased at too dear a price. Persecution had slackened after 1672, but had been renewed in 1683, when Charles found no sympathy with Roman Catholics amongst Dissenters.[3] The insurrection of Monmouth in 1685 brought terrible suffering on many Baptists of the west of England who were among his supporters. The execution of two grandsons of Kiffin (a leading Baptist of his time) has been described in detail by Macaulay, who quotes the remark of Judge Jeffreys, "You have a grandfather who deserves to be hanged as richly as you". Macaulay has made famous also the burning of another Baptist, Elizabeth Gaunt, who anticipated Howard by her visitation of prisoners in jails, her only offence being the sheltering of one of the rebels, who turned king's evidence against her.

Baptists and other Nonconformists have to thank the pro-Romanist policy of James on the one hand, and the common fear of Roman Catholicism on the other, for their deliverance from the persecution of the Restoration period. "Crown and Church were bidding against each other for Nonconformist support. The Crown offered religious toleration and

[1] Gee and Hardy, *op. cit.*, cxviii. [2] *Ibid.* cxx.
[3] Whitley, *op. cit.*, p. 145.
[4] *History of England*, I chap. v.

civic equality by illegal Declarations of Indulgence suspending the obnoxious statutes. The Church promised religious toleration, secured by statute, as soon as a free Parliament should meet."[1] The latter won, and the outcome was the Toleration Act of 1689.[2] Its principle was not the repeal of any of the existent statutes against Dissenters, but exemption from their operation provided prescribed oaths were taken. concern for the abolition of slavery.[5] There were already with certain exceptions. If there was conscientious objection to the taking of an oath, a declaration of political loyalty and of faith in the Holy Trinity, with an acknowledgment of the inspiration of Scripture, might be substituted. Public worship might be celebrated by Dissenters in any certified place, with unlocked doors. This Act defined the legal position of Dissenters for the whole of the eighteenth century and the earliest part of the nineteenth. The Conventicle Act was not repealed until 1813, the Test Act not until 1828.

However limited and grudging this recognition of the rights of the individual conscience may seem to us to-day, it was in the seventeenth century a great victory for the protagonists of liberty. It was the product of many factors, as all great movements inevitably are. But the ultimately decisive factor in history is not the folly of infatuated rulers, the animosity of men smarting under a sense of past injustice, the vested interests of a caste, but the way in which men individually face and ultimately control all these and many other "blind" forces. Throughout the seventeenth century, as we have seen, and from their earliest existence, Baptists had demanded that liberty for religious worship which had to be granted, for the whole nation's sake, before the century closed, Baptists were the first in this country to make this demand, and they had taken their full share of the battle, both in the literal and in the figurative sense. Their claim was now vindicated; they had the legal right to exist, if not much more. What would they make of their newly acquired liberty? The answer of the greater part of the eighteenth century is distinctly disappointing, for this was a period of relative stagnation in the history of the Baptists. It might seem, at first sight, as if they had nothing vital to live for,

[1] Trevelyan, *op. cit.*, p. 470.
[2] Gee and Hardy, *op. cit.*, cxxiii.

PASSION OF THE BAPTISTS FOR LIBERTY

having won the right to exist, so that those would be justified who turn Burke's famous phrase about "the dissidence of dissent"[1] into a suggestion of dissent for the pleasure of dissenting, its *raison d'être* perishing with the occasion of the protest. But like many another equally superficial view, the real causes of the religious stagnation of the earlier eighteenth century lie deeper, and affect all the Churches alike. The decline in the passion of the Baptists for liberty, which left them content so long with a merely "tolerated" existence,[2] corresponds with, and is linked to, an equally marked decline in their evangelistic spirit. Deliverance was to come from other quarters, and even when the Evangelical Revival brought new religious life to the Churches, the Baptists were by no means the most responsive to it. But it is significant that English Baptist sympathies were with the colonists in the American War of Independence,[3] whilst American Baptist soldiers and chaplains took a share in it comparable with that taken by English Baptists in Cromwell's army.[4]

It was natural, indeed inevitable, that the revival of missionary interest amongst the Baptists in 1792, which introduces a new period in their history, should bring with it concern for the abolition of slavery.[5] There were already (from 1784) Baptist Churches amongst the negroes of Jamaica at the time when missionaries were first sent out by the Baptist Missionary Society to that island. Slavery still continued, though the slave trade had been abolished within the British dominions by Acts of 1807 and 1811, as a result of the movement initiated by Clarkson and Wilberforce. A further movement for the abolition of slavery itself was just beginning

---

[1] Speech on Conciliation with the Colonies, March 22, 1775.

[2] It ought to be said that Baptists were represented amongst the "Dissenting Deputies" of Churches in the London area, elected in 1732, for political action to repeal the Test and Corporation Acts, though they were unsuccessful for nearly a century. Subscription to the Anglican Articles was no longer required after 1779, but from 1757 till 1836 all marriages, except those of Quakers, had to be performed at the parish church.

[3] See the last paragraph of the study of J. C. Ryland (Chapter II, p. 72).

[4] Newman, *History of the Baptist Churches in the United States*, pp. 261, 279, etc.; cf. Whitley, *op. cit.*, p. 234.

[5] The honour of being pioneers in this movement belongs to the Society of Friends; cf. the impressive *Journal* of John Woolman (1720-72).

in parliamentary circles when Thomas Burchell and William Knibb were sent out (1823 and 1824) as missionaries to Jamaica. Their advocacy of the interests of the slaves involved them in the bitter animosity of the planters, bringing with it the destruction of missionary property and even peril to the missionaries' lives in connection with an outbreak of slaves in 1831. Knibb, returning to England in 1832, aroused keen indignation by his passionate denunciation of slavery, and led the Baptist contribution[1] to the public feeling which was expressed in the Act of 1833 ; under this Act slavery was terminated by a transitional period of apprenticeship which expired in 1838.

Throughout the nineteenth century Baptists took their full part along with the other Free Churches in the further attainment of political and religious liberty. The political differences of the two great parties corresponded with the religious difference of Churchmen and Dissenters. Some of the landmarks in the struggle, in addition to the repeal of the "Clarendon Code", were the abolition of compulsory Church rates in 1868, the opening of parish churchyards in 1880, the opening of the Universities of Oxford and Cambridge to Dissenters in 1854-56, the abolition of theological tests for official posts at these Universities in 1871. A keen interest was taken by many Baptists in the movement for the disestablishment of the Anglican Church, promoted especially by the "Liberation" Society from 1844; the Irish Church was disestablished in 1868, and the Welsh in 1920. Whilst Baptists still feel that the "establishment" of one religious denomination above all others is an anomaly under present conditions, they are probably less disposed to-day to promote political action for its removal, and prefer to leave this, in the interests of religion, to the more or less inevitable course of events, within and without the Anglican Church. A great source of conflict has been the place of religion in elementary education from the time of its wide extension in 1870. The Act of 1902, which did so much to unify and improve secondary education, aroused great opposition amongst Free Churchmen generally because of the rate-aid given under it to Church "Voluntary" schools. In this, as in many other similar movements, the outstanding Free Churchman was a

[1] Knibb gave evidence before Parliamentary Committees for six days. (*A Memoir of William Knibb*, by J. J. Smith, p. 43.)

Baptist, John Clifford, who might be most fitly described as a soldier of liberty, religious and political. To him all things were moral,[1] and the distinction of sacred and profane changed its meaning into that between the good and the evil. Like Horace Bushnell and F. W. Robertson, he found his way to "a God of Right",[2] and this emphasis explains his eager "political dissent" as well as his ardent religious evangelism. His passion for freedom led him to oppose the South African War of 1899, as it equally led him to support with all his great influence the war of 1914. No man had more fully earned the right to say "Freedom is the breath of a nation's life, and it is only as freedom is granted that it is possible for us to face our difficulties and master them, to understand our problems and find the true solution of them. And of all the liberties we should fight for there is no liberty so great and so absolutely essential as liberty of conscience".[3]

Viscount Grey, in a lecture on "The National Genius of England",[4] once said that the quality which had most helped the race in its development was the power of the passion for individual liberty, combined with a sense of the necessity of order. When we think of the religious and ecclesiastical expression of these outstanding qualities, we naturally think of the Anglican Church as the representative of *order* in this country; we shall not be less true to historic facts in claiming that the Baptist Church has consistently and from the beginning been the representative of the passion for individual *liberty*, and in this has been a pioneer to the other Free Churches of England.

The Baptist tabernacle is not always a graceful structure, but at least we may say this of it, that the twin pillars at its door are evangelism and liberty. This has been its attraction to the men and women of low degree from whom its worshippers have been chiefly drawn. They have found within its walls a living message of the love of God in Christ that has lightened the darkness of their world; the very crudity with which that message has often been stated has made it the more understandable to them. They have also found there a warm sympathy with the toilers of the earth, more difficult

[1] *Life*, by Marchant, p. 193.
[2] *Op. cit.*, p. 24.
[3] *Op. cit.*, p. 226.
[4] As reported in *The Times* of December 13, 1926.

to find, perhaps, within buildings that belong to a higher culture and wider opportunities. The human need for the Gospel, combined with the human instinct for freedom—these have built the Baptist tabernacle.

A fellow-Baptist of wide experience once said to me, "Spurgeon and Clifford together sum up the Baptist denomination". The justice of that remark is most apparent when we consider the outstanding qualities of these two great men, the evangelistic ardour of the "Particular" Baptist, Spurgeon, and the democratic passion of the "General" Baptist, Clifford. Both men aroused strong feelings of dislike in those who differed from their views or lacked sympathy with their "style"; both men were capable of arousing the most devoted personal attachment in those admitted to their intimacy. The "Down-grade Controversy" of 1887-88 showed them characteristically defending their dominant interests, evangelical orthodoxy on the one hand and the rights of Christian freedom on the other.[1] The two men and what they stood for are complementary in any adequate view of the Baptist faith. True evangelism and true liberty are but different applications of the same truth, which is at once eternal life and the maker of all freedom.

A charge sometimes brought against Nonconformity is that it is negative, and therefore has no future. So far as such a charge is sincere, and not a mere trick of debate, catching at a name, it rests on an inadequate knowledge of the history of the last three centuries. Baptists and others opposed the official religion of the State and fought with sword and pen against abuse and tyranny, but they did this for the sake of a positive faith—a faith as definite and as urgent as any for which the Catholic Church has ever stood. Their passion for liberty was ultimately inspired by the supreme positive principle, which stands in contrast with all kinds of emphasis on the external expression of religion—the *intrinsic* authority of the Gospel, which witnesses to itself by its own nature.[2]

The achievement of the liberty for which Baptists and other

---

[1] Accounts of the controversy, from naturally different standpoints, are given in Fullerton's *C. H. Spurgeon*, pp. 310-16, and Marchant's *Dr. John Clifford*, pp. 155-67.

[2] See Chapter IV, 4; also my essay on "The Validity of Christian Experience" in the volume called *The Future of Christianity* (ed. Marchant).

Free Churchmen have contended has brought with it perils of its own. They are now free to enter many doors which once were closed to them; this means that they are the more exposed to the influences of that "worldliness" which their ancestors in the faith denounced. It is a much more difficult thing to maintain the high ideals of the Baptist faith when the Baptist life is no longer more or less secluded. "It is easy in the world to live after the world's opinion; it is easy in solitude to live after our own; but the great man is he who in the midst of the crowd keeps with perfect sweetness the independence of solitude."[1] This truth is often ignored by those whose social environment unconsciously shapes their Christian ethics.

On the other hand, the fact that the external rights of liberty in religious faith and worship have been already won may obscure the vision of those even greater issues which are never fully won. Liberty within is a more difficult attainment than liberty without. Prejudices which we nurture within our own hearts are more subtle and dangerous than those whose folly and injustice we can see plainly when they belong to others. Baptists need to remember, perhaps more than most, that if there is an externalism of Church authority which has worked mischief in religion, there is also an externalism of the appeal to Scripture, not less alien to the living truth of Christ. There are conventions and traditions in the religious life of Baptists which need constant scrutiny by the highest and most spiritual standards lest that which once helped becomes a hindrance to the faith. It is easy to pass resolutions for the amendment of others which nobody will ever take seriously; it is hard to resolve to amend oneself, at the cost, perhaps, of effort and pain. If Baptist life and faith are threatened by a multitude of attractive interests which tend to the loss of earnest simplicity and devotion, we must not forget the tendency of those who still stand in the old ways to misjudge their brethren and to become hardened in the Gospel. There are enemies of the truth as it is in Jesus more subtle than ecclesiastical courts and more stubborn than the most ancient vested interests. There are prejudices and errors of knowledge and judgment within every community which can be overcome only by a struggle as protracted and -

---

[1] Emerson, essay on "Self-Reliance"

patient as that of the past for denominational existence. There is, in fact, an unachieved liberty *within* faith as well as *for* faith, and its best safeguard is found in the dominating principle of that book which this chapter began by quoting, Milton's *Areopagitica*: " Give me the liberty to know, to utter, and to argue freely according to conscience, above all liberties."

VII

THE STRENGTH AND THE WEAKNESS OF THE BAPTISTS

THE great majority of religious men are what they are ecclesiastically because they have grown up in it. This is as it should be, since nothing atones for the absence of those memories of childhood and youth which are progressively hallowed by the faith of the grown man, and gain a richer interpretation by the experience of life. The familiar walls of the church, the familiar phrases of prayer and praise, even the familiar tones of voice of him who first opened to us the way of the Spirit, gain a sacramental quality, so as to be inseparable in memory from the experience they mediated. They have helped to bring us into a living tradition that we might discover " how great a thing it is to live at the end of so many ages, heirs to the thoughts of the wise, the labours of the good, the prayers of the devout ".[1]

Yet it is also true that each of us enters this living stream with his own unique life, his own capacities for emotion ready to be stirred, his own thoughts striving to become articulate, his own will claiming its free exercise. The truth —at least, the truth for *me*—lies in, and is tested by, a personal reaction to this tradition. " Tradition and conscience are the two wings given to the human soul to reach to truth. . . . Where you find the general permanent voice of humanity agreeing with the voice of your conscience, be sure that you hold in your grasp something with absolute truth— gained and for ever yours."[2] This, of course, implies the right and the duty of each to criticize the religious tradition in and through which he lives. Such criticism is the essential condition not only of progress, individual and corporate, but even of clear conviction and intelligent faith. This is true

---

[1] Martineau, *Home Prayers*, p. 6.
[2] Mazzini, quoted by Bolton King, *Mazzini*, pp. 240, 244.

for all religion; it ought to be especially true for those forms of it which emphasize voluntary choice and personal faith as primary duties.

We may often gain much help in the process of examining our own religious faith and practice by learning how it looks to one who stands outside our own communion, provided he be sympathetic, well-informed, and able to give expression to his thinking. Some years before this book was planned, I asked three such competent observers to give me their frank opinions on " The Strength and the Weakness of the Baptists." I summarize their answers, for the sake of brevity. The Congregationalist answered: " Your strength is your correspondence with the original practice of the New Testament and the fact that you make the moral meaning of baptism unmistakable. Your weakness is that all matters of ceremony are secondary to the truths of the Gospel, that your special emphasis is a bar to Christian reunion, and that you lay stress on one side only of the meaning of baptism, i.e. individual faith, whereas it also symbolizes divine grace." The Wesleyan answered: " Your strength is your devotion to evangelical truth, and rich Christian experience, and your willingness to bear criticism about baptism. Your weakness is theological narrowness and excessive individualism, the lack of a connexional system, so that the ministers of smaller Churches suffer, and too little use is made of lay preachers, and the undue emphasis implied in the name ' Baptist', for which, of course, you are not to blame." The Quaker said: " Your strength is your evangelical emphasis, your open and public confession of faith, with definite and dramatic entrance into the Church, the stress on personal decision, and the stand for supremacy of conscience. Your weakness is your theological narrowness, your Scriptural literalism, the making baptism essential to Church membership, the want of a circuit system which would bring in more lay ministry, and the lack of sufficiently definite Christian teaching to young people." The general justice of these criticisms would be admitted by many Baptists, and the practical agreement is significant. The strength of Baptists lies in their Scriptural individualism, their weakness chiefly in the defects of their quality. We cannot emphasize one word in a sentence without running the risk of slurring over other words; we cannot emphasize one truth without the risk of inadequate attention to other truths, as history has repeatedly taught.

The direct appeal to the authority of Scripture is common to all the Protestant Churches, but there is a special motive for the Baptist use of it. Baptists are continually thrown back on the Bible to justify what seems to many a strange and arbitrary idiosyncrasy. But intelligent use of the Bible to justify the baptism of believers trains men in the intelligent use of the Bible for other purposes, teaches them to look up things for themselves, and to trust no reports at second-hand —a habit which is always one mark of a good student. Such direct use of the Bible serves to bring men into touch with the experience it records, and often into that intuitive experience in which God and man are face to face. The value of such Bible-reading is great; there can be hardly any more serious feature of the religious life of to-day than the very marked decline in it—a decline which, unfortunately, Baptists also exhibit.

On the other hand, the very simplicity and directness of this use of Scripture brings its own perils. The individual believer is encouraged to interpret it for himself, but he often lacks the most elementary training for this. The prejudice of ignorance borrows the strength of genuine religious conviction, and sometimes issues in a papal dogmatism. Baptists as a whole are often wanting in any sense of history, whether the history of the thousand years in which the experience behind the Bible slowly deposited itself in the literary record, or those intervening centuries of the history of the Church which have added so much to the interpretation of the Bible. It may be admitted that this is a defect in some degree common to many Churches, but other Churches have silent correctives of overweening confidence which Baptists lack— such as the respect for education amongst the Presbyterians, or the long and rich perspective of the parish church and the Prayer Book amongst the Anglicans. Whilst "Fundamentalism" as a belligerent movement has relatively little hold amongst Baptists of this country, there is still a good deal of suspicion of even the moderate amount of Biblical scholarship which has been more or less assimilated by most other Churches. Yet Baptists, of all people, ought to welcome that criticism which takes men back beyond the letter to the living spirit, and unbares the experience which was first creative of the literature. Fortunately, the Baptist love of liberty comes in to correct the tendencies of assertive literalism and eschatological vagary, and heresy-hunters are not popular with a Baptist Union Assembly.

The real strength of the emphasis on individual experience (see Chapter III) has already been exhibited, and need not be further developed, except to say that it brings men face to face with God in Christ. This makes the intrinsic nature of His Gospel, as known in experience, the ultimate authority—indeed, the only authority in the real sense, for " God is love " and the Gospel of His love is the revelation of His nature, and what further testimonial does God ever need? But the connected weakness found alongside of this strength amongst Baptists needs careful thought, for it affects the whole conception of the Church and the life of the Church. It does not seem to me too much to say that Baptists as Churchmen are still largely dominated by an eighteenth-century philosophy of society, disguised under their traditional interpretation of Scripture. That pronounced individualist, Jean Jacques Rousseau, discussed the social forms of life as if they were the arbitrary and voluntary creation of a number of unitary individuals, instead of being the cradle in which the individual life is nurtured and the breast at which it sucks. Similarly, it is possible to talk of conversion and the work of the Holy Spirit as if it occurred in a social vacuum, in order that a number of unitary products might subsequently be brought together to form a Church. But this ignores the fact that in personality there are the two elements of individuality and sociality growing side by side from the very beginning, and not less in religious than in biological and cultural and moral developments. The family is already a social environment, and without it there could be no individual life, yet it is possible for a Baptist to write, " fatherhood and sonship are relations expressive of individual and not of corporate experiences ".[1]

How can there be a father before there is a son, or a son before there is a father? The truth is rather that the social relation implied in fatherhood and sonship is just as much a capacity of personality as the individual consciousness. If it were not for such relationship as the family and the clan

[1] Mullins, *The Axioms of Religion*, p. 39.

and the State imply there could be no development of the individual consciousness at all. These things are, of course, the commonplaces of sociology to-day, but they are singularly ignored in many discussions of the "separated" Church. The only difference is that the application in this case is to man's highest interests. The Church is not an arbitrary "extra", a sort of religious club he may choose to join; it is the crowning religious expression of that sociality which is part of his very constitution. Because it is that, it becomes the temple of the Holy Spirit in larger ways that the individual temple of a single life can offer. It is unreasonable to contrast the work of the Holy Spirit in the individual life and in the social group as if there could be any rivalry; these realms are complementary and closely—indeed inseparably—interwoven. Baptists must and will continue to stand for the truth of a regenerated Church membership expressed in believers' baptism; but they will never make that testimony as effective as it ought to be till they have added to it a nobler Church-consciousness, and a profounder sense of the whole group, as well as of the individual life, as the arena of the Spirit's activity.[1] It belonged to them in the earlier days, when the Church was identified with the narrow group of "true" believers, and the world lay without; it has gradually grown dim—except for a few old-fashioned Churches—through the increasing relation of the "believer" with that outside world, and his recognition that the old distinction of "saved" and "lost" is no longer possible—at any rate, in its old sense and scope. A nobler Church-consciousness can come only through a new conception of the Church—such a conception, for example, as that which runs through the Epistle to the Ephesians. At the risk of saying something that may be misunderstood by those within and those without, I would say quite deliberately that Baptists need an "Oxford Movement" of *their own order,* so as to give their truth of an individual relation to God its complementary truth of a social relation to Him. Such a movement would doubtless bring some changes in worship and in polity, not those changes which are like new patches on an old garment,

---

[1] This must not be taken to ignore the fine achievements of Baptists in voluntary giving, for work at home and abroad, to which reference is made elsewhere—the more remarkable because this has been done in the absence of any "connexional" system.

but those true changes of a living development in which the unity is not lost.[1]

The third point in which both the strength and the weakness of the Baptists may be discerned relates to believers' baptism itself, and brings to a focus what has just been said about the relation to the Bible and to the Church. The first and foremost contribution of Baptists to the Church Catholic is like that of the Hebrew prophets—the essential and primary place of the moral within the religious. The moral change wrought in genuine conversion, the personal repentance and faith which are the religious features of that conversion, the open confession which commits the life to a new purpose—these great truths are admirably and forcibly expressed in believers' baptism by immersion, and expressed as no other Church expresses them. All this is New Testament faith and practice. But it is not the whole faith of the New Testament.

Does not baptism express much more than a personal act? Is it not, *by virtue of being that,* the New Testament door of entrance into a life of supernatural energies, the surrender to that "Law of the Spirit" which the Apostle set in strongest contrast to the common life of men? Let any Baptist, with an open mind, set himself to study the New Testament references to baptism, and he will perhaps be surprised to find how closely it is related to the gift of the Holy Spirit. The baptism of John expressed a moral decision; the baptism of Christ is sharply contrasted with this, as a baptism with or in the Holy Spirit. There is the same contrast in the conversation of Christ with Nicodemus, when entrance into the Kingdom is made conditional of being "born of water and the Spirit". That Paul closely related water-baptism and that which it symbolized is evident, for "in one Spirit were we all baptized into one body . . . and were all made to drink of one Spirit ". If the descent into the waters of baptism meant death and burial with Christ, in that mystical union with Him which carries with it death unto sin, not less did it mean to Paul the ascent into new life, defined by him as newness of "Spirit". The Colossians are reminded not only that they were buried with Christ in their baptism, but that they were raised with Christ in the same baptism, the

[1] Something has already been said in Chapter I on the difficulty, yet discipline, of the practical reconciliation of individual conviction and social tradition within the Church. See also p. 85.

power of the new life working through their faith. It is not without significance that when Paul speaks of the one Body and the one Spirit, he should straightway pass on to speak of the one baptism expressing the one faith which unites to the one Lord, "The Lord the Spirit", as he elsewhere says. Thus, to be baptized into Christ is to put on Christ, i.e. to enter that realm of the Spirit over which Christ is Lord.

It needs to be said, of course, that the connection between water-baptism and the baptism of the Spirit is of no mechanical kind, such as quasi-magical ideas of the ceremony would suggest. The Spirit-baptism of Cornelius and his friends preceded their water-baptism; in fact, the water-baptism was administered to these Gentiles (without precedent) on the ground that they had already received the gift which it expressed. The group of disciples at Ephesus who had not received the Holy Spirit at the time of their "Johannine" baptism were baptized again into the name of the Lord Jesus, and after Paul had laid his hands upon them, the gift hitherto withheld was given. But these are mentioned as exceptional cases. The recipient of baptism in the New Testament times normally expected to be the recipient of the spiritual powers of the new life which he entered by his baptism. There could be no risk of encouraging the idea of "baptismal regeneration" (in the modern sense), because *all who were baptized were already believers*, i.e. the moral and spiritual conditions of their personal faith became the real channel of the Spirit's highest energies. Indeed, it was the very divorce of baptism from personal faith which has made "sacramentarianism" possible.

Let us try to enter into the experience of a believer baptized in those first days, using the interpretative reconstruction of a scholar who stands outside the present issue:—

In baptism (of course, adult) something happened. Faith had been there before, receptiveness toward the good news of Christ. The Divine Spirit had been already present, taking of the things of Christ and showing them to the believer. But now, once for all, the convert made his own the movings of the Divine love in his heart. And thus there would come to him in his baptism a wonderful spiritual quickening, a new enhancing of the power and grasp of faith, a fresh realization of communion with the once crucified and now risen Lord. Hence, there is good ground for the statement of von Dobschütz that "according to the early

Christian view we may speak of real effects of baptism in the sense that here the person does not give himself something by his activity, but God gives him what he has only to receive." [1]

Baptists have been reluctant to recognize this "baptismal grace", just because, in their judgment, it is utterly misrepresented and distorted when ascribed to unconscious infants. The reaction from a false doctrine of divine grace in baptism has made them suspicious even of the genuine sacramentalism of the New Testament. We have been saying *believers'* baptism so emphatically that we have failed, or at least are failing now, to say with anything like equal emphasis, believers' *baptism*, i.e. the entrance of believers into a life of supernatural powers.

Here, then, is the present Baptist opportunity, and it is a great one. No other Church has been loyal to the New Testament connection of baptism with personal faith. No other Church, therefore, could give so forcible a testimony to the work of the Spirit on the believer, which is not less emphatically linked with baptism in the New Testament. If any Baptist reader is afraid that this may mean a sacramentalism of the lower kind, with consecrated water rather than the evangelical truth in the heart of the believer as the primary medium of the Spirit, let it be said quite distinctly that I am pleading for the connection of water-baptism with the Spirit in exactly the sense in which all Baptists plead for its connection with personal faith. If the New Testament teaches the latter, it assuredly also teaches the former, and Baptists are really committed to both. If appeal be made to such a word as the Apostle's "Received ye the Spirit by the works of the law, or by the hearing of faith?", the answer is that undoubtedly personal faith is the realm of the Spirit's activity, but the confession of that faith in believers' baptism brought a new opportunity for divine grace, because it was itself an act of personal faith.

Though this book is not a history of the Baptists, enough has been said of the different types of life within the three centuries to show the great changes that have taken place. Doubtless other changes equally great will mark our further development, and no man can foresee them. But at the present time, and in this country, the Baptist future seems to depend on the relation to the distinctive feature of believers'

[1] H. A. A. Kennedy, *St. Paul and the Mystery Religions*, p. 249.

baptism. Baptists must make either more or less of it. If they make less of it, they will be absorbed into Congregationalism, and their distinctive testimony and consciousness will be lost—a result I should greatly deplore. If they make more of it, it must be along the line indicated of a greater spiritual content, and not simply of a literalistic appeal to the Bible. Believers will not be deterred from baptism by immersion if they are taught the rich and full meaning given to it by the New Testament.

Apart from this characteristic feature (and all it implies) the future of the Baptists is bound up with the future of the evangelical faith. The presentation of that faith, in order to be successful, has always to be in terms of contemporary thought and life. This is true even when the presentation is antithetical, or perhaps we should say that its especial truth is then seen. Thus, at the present time, the fundamental need is for a clear assertion of the reality of religion over against the modern challenge that religion is a subjective illusion. Here the primary Baptist emphasis should be on the appeal to experience, that experience of obedience to the will of God which brings the proof of the teaching that it is of God. The central truth of the evangelical faith is the sacrificial love of God realized in the grace of Christ. Over against the idea of a passive or absent God, or a God fettered by the "laws" of His universe, we have to teach that God is active, present, redeeming, and that man, by His grace, may have a direct relation of fellowship with Him. All revivals of religion are in essence due to the realization that God is much nearer than we thought. Further, the Baptist emphasis on conversion asserts moral responsibility and human freedom over against the naturalism and determinism of the past generation (themselves profoundly shaken by the new physics). Most of all there is needed a new and clear teaching of the doctrine of the Holy Spirit, as against the rationalism that rejects all mystery, and the externalism which materializes mystery into manageable forms. The true emphasis is that of the New Testament—on personal faith as the human condition of divine activity, which is the truth supremely expressed in believers' baptism.[1]

---

[1] See A. C. Underwood, *Conversion: Christian and Non-Christian*, for an excellent account of baptism as "The Dramatic Representation of Regeneration" (chap. ix).

APPENDIX I

THE FINAL AUTHORITY[1]

A Baptist minister[2], after more than a quarter of a century's pastoral work in Baptist Churches, tells us that all through this period his mind was disturbed by the haunting question, "By what authority doest thou these things?" Finally, he settled his doubts and difficulties by accepting the authority of the Church of Rome:—

> "The externals of the Church, if the expression may be allowed, never appealed to me. What did appeal, and overwhelmingly appeal, was its historic descent, its firm and authoritative foundation, and the reality of its presence in the world as the 'Body,' the very Voice, of the Living Christ . . . . the only foundation and pillar of the truth, the only interpreter of the 'revelation', the only guardian of the Faith once delivered to the Saints."

This is not the place to enter on any criticism of this appeal to history. History is a two-edged tool, and it can destroy that which it is taken up to defend. It is sufficient for our present purpose, which is positive and constructive, to note this as a clear and actual example of the transference of loyalties from the individual authority of personal conviction to the social authority of a community, from the Bible as interpreted by the individual, to the Bible as finally and authoritatively interpreted by the Church. Of course, the challenging question has a far wider application than to ministerial status and of service in any one denomination. It ought to be put by every Christian to himself, whatever his particular vocation, and whatever be the Church to which he belongs. Some answer to it is essential to any intelligent response of faith, and to any adequate

---

[1] As stated in the preface to this new addition, Dr. Robinson proposed to add a new chapter with this title. The draft here printed was the last piece of work he accomplished. He put it into my hands when he had to be moved to a Nursing Home, but as he was unable to go through it, even in typescript, it has been included here as an appendix.—E.A.P.

[2] J. F. Makepeace, whose *All I could never be* (Blackwell, 1924) describes this development (1872-1912). The passage cited occurs pp. 111-112.

acceptance of revelation. In fact, the answer must affect our whole conception of what revelation is, both in content and method. Our very philosophy of revelation is often a more or less rationalized form of our individual contact with the Beyond. It is natural enough that we should emphasize the particular media which have been the " means of grace " to ourselves. They become our most individualised sacrament, however trivial their occasion and origin. In them the temporal form acquires an eternal content. But, in putting the question to ourselves, we must not be content to answer it simply by a choice between the Bible and the Church. That is far too superficial an answer, however popular it may be. The truth lies deeper, and like all historical data, is much more complex. Both individual conviction and the authority of a community are involved in any and every religious decision, whilst in every profession, Protestant or Roman Catholic, both Bible and Church are involved, and essentially involved. The difference is in the ultimate emphasis, and a difference of emphasis can easily become a difference of kind. (In fact, most of the differences of human life could be explained as differences of emphasis.)

In the Baptist life and faith, as has been described in this book, the emphasis clearly falls on the side of the individual conviction. The rite of baptism is, as in the New Testament, administered only to those who take the initiative in making a personal profession of faith. The Church is avowedly constituted of believers who have been individually convinced of the truth of that which they profess. The most essential aspect of the ministerial vocation is not any prescribed rite or ceremony, but individual vocation. The gifts and fruit of the Holy Spirit are far oftener conceived in their individual relations to the believer than as corporately conditioned. It would, however, be quite wrong to ignore the influence of a corporate tradition running through all this. Most of those who " spontaneously " avow the Baptist form of faith on the basis of individual conviction have, in fact, grown up in a Baptist environment. Consciously or unconsciously, they have been subjected to Baptist influences from their earliest days. Those influences are a particular form of the common evangelical tradition. This claims, and rightly claims, to set forth and employ important elements of Biblical truth. But, not less than any other form of tradition, though in different ways, " it depends chiefly for its active propagation on the continuity of a community in and by which it is cherished. Baptist life and faith may indeed be, as we have seen (Chapter VII), criticised for not making enough of the factors of community, and no purely individualistic reply to this kind of criticism would be adequate. But the community-factors are there, and inevitably there."

Similar things hold true of the Roman Catholic tradition, though the other way round, and in much more systematized fashion. The child, already received into the Church by its baptism, normally grows through and into a tradition which is transformed into a habit, and becomes "second nature." The social side of human personality thus receives fullest recognition from the very outset of life. The element or factor of personal conviction, however, is not ignored, but remains more or less latent until individual responsibility can exert itself. Then, the tradition made familiar by long habit is consciously accepted and continued, or there may be a deliberate rejection or neglect of it, and a man goes out into the wilderness of the unfamiliar. In a "conversion" to Roman Catholicism, the emphasis falls yet more clearly on personal decision (made under the guidance of the Holy Spirit)[1].

In all this, the place assigned to the Church is manifest, and it becomes explicit in the decrees of the Council of Trent. But the warning already given must be remembered. The decrees do not set the Church in direct antithesis to the Bible. All that is claimed (and it is a sufficiently comprehensive "all") is that the Church has been divinely authorised to interpret the Bible. Such a claim fully endows the tradition with all that it needs to make it *de jure* as well as *de facto*. This authority to interpret belongs to the divine purpose, and the Church, in effect at least, becomes the final authority. The initial question is answered—by the transference of responsibility to other people.

It is plain, then, that acceptance of the authority of revelation does not resolve itself into a simple choice between the conviction of the believer and that of the religious community. There is a new product[2] and since both factors are involved, a place must be found for both in our philosophy of revelation. This is a far-reaching subject, and I can do little more here than refer to the larger book in which I have tried to deal with it.[3] The path of understanding takes us from any thought of the individual and the community in isolation to the fuller recognition of their unity in the hands of God, and in the operation of His providence. As, indeed, in all the normal

[1] A classical expression of this is known to all in Newman's "Lead, kindly Light."
[2] We may illustrate by the most familiar examples in nature, viz. oxygen and hydrogen continuing to give water as their product. At a higher level we have the union of soul and body, spirit and matter, in personality.
[3] *Redemption and Revelation* (1942).

developments of life; and not only in those attaching to religion, the community is essential for the training and preparation of the individual, and the individual to the constant renewal of the community. At some point, the conscious contact of the two will raise the question as to which should be uppermost in authority ; the answer decides a man's ecclesiastical choice. But he will never wholly escape from the factor which he subordinates, since he is characterized by both individuality and sociality. In their divinely wrought unity they exert their dual authority, and the Bible stands out from history as the unique record of man's converse with God, and of God's converse with man. As such the Bible will exert its proper authority, and on sufficient grounds it rules to its own degree intrinsically, simply by being what it is.

One confirmation that we are on the right path in thus thinking of the authority of revelation is that the whole development becomes a training in moral responsibility. All along the individual learns to make decisions, and not the least in the culminating one. God uses in revelation the methods familiar to us in all true education, the aim being the evocation of personality. But these methods are those of the invitation or pressure of the community, which becomes the great and necessary corrective of individual wilfulness or ignorance.

The final authority must always be God, but He has many media, and supreme amongst them all is the life, death and resurrection of His Son, Jesus Christ, proclaimed by the Church, and within the fellowship of the Holy Spirit, to which the witness of the Spirit within the believer testifies.

H. W. R.

APPENDIX II

SELECTED BIBLIOGRAPHY

The earliest Baptist historians were Crosby (1738-40), Ivimey (1811-30) and Taylor (1818). Evans (1862-64) and Cramp (1875) produced useful studies, but their work must now be supplemented by the extensive documentary material made available of recent decades both by the secular and the ecclesiastical historians. The standard modern history is W. T. Whitley, *A History of British Baptists* (1923, second edition 1932). For Scotland and America add *A History of the Baptists in Scotland* (ed. by Geo. Yuille, 1926) and A. H. Newman, *A History of the Baptist Churches in the United States* (sixth edition, 1915). *The Baptist Quarterly* and *The Chronicle* (published quarterly by the American Baptist Historical Society) continue to make important contributions to the study of Baptist history. There is also value in the briefer general accounts of H. C. Vedder, *A Short Baptist History* (1897), J. T. Christian, *A History of the Baptists* (Nashville, 1922), G. O. Griffith, *A Pocket History of the Baptist Movement* (1929) and A. C. Underwood, *A History of the English Baptists* (1946).

The Baptist movement on the Continent of Europe may be studied in J. H. Rushbrooke, *The Baptist Movement on the Continent of Europe* (1923) and *Some Chapters of European Baptist History* (1929). H. Gieselbusch (ed.), *Um die Gemeinde Ausgewählte-Schriften von Julius Köbner*, (Berlin, 1927), R. Baresel, *Julius Köbner* (Kassel, 1930) and Hans Luckey, *Johann Gerhard Oncken und die Anfänge des deutschen Baptismus* (Kassel, 1934) represent the beginnings of the scientific study of German Baptist origins.

A number of important Reports have been issued of recent years defining the Baptist attitude to modern ecclesiastical issues. Particular attention may be called to "The Baptist Reply to the Lambeth Appeal" (1926), "The Report of the Special Committee appointed by the Baptist Union Council on the question of union between Baptists, Congregationalists and Presbyterians" (1937), and to two Reports submitted to the Atlanta World Congress in 1939: "The Baptist Contribution to Christian Unity" and "The Reports and Findings of the Oxford and Edinburgh Conferences." The full Reports of the Baptist World Congresses contain important material dealing with varied aspects of Baptist life and thought.

McGlothlin, *Baptist Confessions of Faith* (1910) opens up an important field of study. Baptist theories of the Church, Ministry and Sacraments are treated in H. Wheeler Robinson, *Baptist Principles* (1925), A. Dakin, *The Baptist View of the Church and Ministry* (1944), E. A. Payne *The Fellowship of Believers: Baptist Thought and Practice Yesterday and To-day* (1945) and R. C. Walton, *The Gathered Community* (1946). Two other books by the last named set the Baptist contribution in the larger framework of modern Church (1944) and *The Church Awakes: the Story of the Modern Missionary Movement* (1942).

Other books on special topics that deserve notice are H. S. Burrage, *Baptist Hymnwriters and Their Hymns* (1888), Carey Bonner, *Some Baptist Hymnists* (1937), J. H. Shakespeare, *Baptist and Congregational Pioneers* (1905), L. F. Brown, *Baptists and the Fifth Monarchy Movement* (1912), as well as a number of important studies of local Baptist history.

E. A. P.

APPENDIX III

SUMMARY OF BAPTIST STATISTICS

Taken from the *Summary of Statistics,* 1940 published by the Baptist World Alliance.

Continent	Churches	Pastors and Missionaries	Members	Sunday Scholars
EUROPE (1)	5,357	3,930	660,881	508,633
ASIA	4,786	1,939	479,174	210,635
AFRICA	1,952	535	118,330	46,540
AMERICA:				
North	58,156	43,293	10,931,936	7,155,960
Central and West Indies...	752	564	74,099	66,312
South	733	497	62,978	58,015
AUSTRALIA and NEW ZEALAND	527	460	40,716	47,789
Totals (1)	72,263	51,218	12,368,114	(2)8,093,884

NOTES.

(1) This excludes the U.S.S.R., where two strong groups, the "All-Union of Baptists" and the "All-Union of Evangelical Christians," merged into a single Union in 1944. Both are uncomprisingly Baptist, and more than twenty years earlier (both being already members of the Baptist World Alliance) had accepted a common declaration of faith and order. Precise and certified reports of their membership are not yet available; they themselves in a published statement (1942) asserted that they number four millions, but it is uncertain whether this figure represents community strength or church membership. In any case their inclusion would very substantially increase the total.

(2) Owing to the impossibility of obtaining complete figures during war-time, the Alliance has issued no statistical statement since 1940. Sufficient reports, however, have reached its office to indicate that the total membership—with the U.S.S.R. still omitted—is in 1945 well over thirteen millions.

Baptists are now the largest Free Church communion in the world. The Methodists, who report, according to Dr. Newton Flew in *A Christian Year Book,* 1945 (p. 50), 11,666,646 communicant members, are nearest to them in numbers.

J. H. R.

INDEX

I.—PERSONS

Allen, William, 27, 32–36, 127, 128
Angus, Joseph, 86, 102
Arnold, Thomas, 38n.
Arthington, Robert, 116n.

Barrow, Humphrey, 42
Beddome, Benjamin, 56
Bentley, Holman, 116, 120
Booth, Abraham, 100
Bromehead, Hugh and Anne, 96
Brown, John Turland, 111
Browne, Robert, 12
Bunyan, John, 16, 20, 28, 41, 52, 60, 75, 100, 130
Burchell, Thomas, 134
Busher, Leonard, 125

Calvin, John, 94
Carey, William, 15, 63–64, 111, 113–115, 119
Carlyle, Thomas, 32, 36, 128n.
Celsus, 110
Cheare, Abraham, 27, 30, 40
Clifford, John, 15, 25, 135–136
Comber, Thomas, 116
Cromwell, Henry, 34
Cromwell, Oliver, 14, 26, 33–36, 123, 127, 128, 129
Crosley, David, 42, 46–47

Deane, Richard, 127
Denne, Henry, 112n.
Denney, James, 98
Dutton, Ann, 25, 50–56, 112

Emerson, R. W., 137

Fairbairn, A. M., 23, 95
Fawcett, John, 68
Foskett, Bernard, 57–58
Foster, John, 25, 66
Fuller, Andrew, 112, 113, 115

Gardiner, S. R., 35, 36
Gaunt, Elizabeth, 131
Gore, Bishop, 103
Gough, William, 128
Grant, William, 54
Grenfell, George, 116, 120
Grey, Viscount, 36n., 135

Hall, Robert, 15, 64–68, 100, 111
Harrison, Thomas, 127
Headlam, Bishop, 103
Helwys, Thomas, 13, 124, 125, 126
Holles, Denzil, 32
Hooker, Richard, 99
Hort, F. J. A., 103n.
Huish, Deborah, 33
Hunt, John, 51
Hutchinson, John, 127

James, William, 79n.
Jones, Stanley, 119

Keach, Benjamin, 38–41, 48, 49
Kennedy, H. A. A., 146
Kiffin, William, 100, 131
Kinghorn, Joseph, 67, 100
Klausner, Joseph, 108
Knibb, William, 15, 115, 134
Knollys, Hanserd, 39, 41
Krishna Pal, 119

Lacey, T. A., 102
Lambe, Thomas, 36–38
Laud, Archbishop, 126, 128n.
Lightfoot, Bishop, 103
Lilburne, Robert, 127
Lindsay, T. M. 16, 87
Ludlow, Edmund, 127
Luther, Martin, 16
Lytton, Bulwer-, 68

Maclaren, Alexander, 15
Macgregor, W. M., 103
Marshman, Joshua, 115, 119
Martineau, James, 98n., 139
Mazzini, Joseph, 139
Meynell, Alice, 22
Milton, John, 123n., 138
Mitchell, William, 46
Moore, John, 52, 53
Mullins, E. Y., 24, 93, 142
Murton, John, 12n., 125

Newman, Cardinal, 88n, 95
Newman, William, 56

Penn, William, 94
Pepys, Samuel, 25

Richard, Timothy, 117, 119, 120
Rippon, John, 57, 60
Robinson, John, 13
Robinson, Robert, 100
Rousseau, Jean Jacques, 142
Rushbrooke, J. H., 12n.
Rutherford, Samuel, 52
Ryland, John, 64, 100, 110
Ryland, John Collett, 56–65, 100, 113

Saker, Alfred, 116
Sanday, William, 69
Skepp, John, 42, 53
Skippon, Philip, 32
Smyth, John, 12, 13, 73, 88, 96, 105, 124, 126, 127
Spurgeon, Charles Haddon, 15, 25, 100, 111, 136
Steadman, William, 121
Steed, Robert, 42, 43, 46, 48–49
Steele, Ann, 55n.
Strudwick, John, 46
Swete, H. B., 71n.

Thomas, John, 114, 120
Trevelyan, George Macaulay, 16, 128n., 129 and n., 132

Venner, Thomas, 17n., 128
Vernon, Caleb, 25–32
Vernon, John, 25–32, 33, 35

Ward, William, 115, 119
Wesley, Charles, 60–61
Wheeler, Francis, 111
Wheeler, John, 110–111
Whitefield, George, 47, 50n.
Whitley, W. T., vii, 32 et passim
Williams, Charles, 100
Williams, Roger, 27, 121, 125
Wyclif, John, 15

Zwingli, Ulrich, 99

II.—SUBJECTS

Alliance, Baptist World, 92-93
Anabaptists, 12, 72, 126
Apostolical Succession, 103
Apprentices, 44-45, 111
Arminianism, 14, 60-61, 101, 112, 126
Associations, 91, 92, 107, 121

Baptism—
  Believers', 13-14, 16, 18, 29-30, 69-75, 97-98, 144-146, 147
  Infant, 71-73, 97-98
  Mode, 13-14, 29-30, 69-71
  Symbolism, 16, 69, 78-80
Baptismal Regeneration, 97-98, 144-146

Baptists—
  American, 14, 17n., 24, 92, 93, 101, 121, 123, 125, 133
  Criticism of, 139-140
  European, 154
  Future of, 136-138, 146-147
  "General," 14, 101, 112, 126
  "New Connexion," 14, 112
  "Particular," 14, 101, 112, 127
Baptist Union Assembly, 83, 92, 107

Bible—
  Authority of, 16, 55-56, 86-87, 140, 141
  Criticism of, 17
  Religion of, 18-21
Boxer massacres, 118
Bristol Baptist College, 57-64, 65
Broadmead Church, Bristol, 130, 131

Bugbrooke Baptist Church, 111

Calvinism, 14, 15, 50, 56, 60, 63, 86, 112, 113
Cameroons, 116
Catholicism, Roman, 126, 131
"Cavalier" Parliament, 129
China, 117, 118
Christ, Headship of, 29, 84, 93, 124, 125

Church—
  Constitution of, 82-88
  Idea of, v, 13, 18-23, 73, 82-84, 85-86, 142-143
  Organizations of, 94
Church-meetings, 88-90
College Lane Church, Northampton, 53, 64, 110
Communion, "open" and "strict," 67, 100
"Communion of saints," 98-99
Communion Service, 77, 97-101
Congo, 116
Conservatism, religious, 137
Conventicle Act, 130, 132
Conversion, 51, 52, 74-77, 84, 144, 147
Corporation Act, 129
Creeds, 78, 79, 80
Cripplegate Church, 41-50, 53

Deacons, 85, 88
Discipline, 42-47, 89, 90
Disestablishment, 134
"Dissenting Deputies," 133n.
Domestic life, 15-16, 44
"Down-grade Controversy," 136

Education controversy, 134
Education, religious, 15–16, 39, 77, 84*n.*
Epiclesis, 99
Evangelicalism, 79, 80, 147
Evangelism, 56, 109–110
Excommunication, 47, 89

"Fifth Monarchy," 17*n.*, 32, 36, 128
Five Mile Act, 131
"Fundamentalism," 17, 141
Funds, denominational, 15, 92, 107*n.*

Great Gransden Church, 54, 55

Heresy, 45, 61, 79, 142
Holiness, 19
Hymn-singing, 41, 48–50, 96
Hyper-Calvinism, 50, 55, 112

Individualism, 76
Indulgence, Declaration of, 131
Introspection, 59

Lambeth "Appeal," reply to, 83
Laymen, 104, 110
Liberty, 119, 123–138
Lollardy, 16
Long Parliament, 126, 129*n.*
Lord's Supper, the, 97–101
Lutheranism, 15

Mass movements, 76, 121
"Messengers," 112
Ministry, 102–107

Missions—
  Foreign, 81, 108–122
  Home, 111–112, 121
Moulton Baptist Church, 111, 113

"Open" membership, 52*n.*, 101
Ordination, 105, 106*n.*

Paulicians, 71
Persecution, 125, 126, 129–132
Petrobrusians, 72
Preaching, 65, 66, 96
Priesthood of all believers, 104
Prophets of Israel, 19, 108
Puritanism, 36, 82, 96, 123, 127, 128–129

Rawdon Baptist College, 121
Reformation, 11, 16, 19
Regent's Park Baptist College, 56

Sacramentalism, 145, 146
Separatism, 13, 45, 126
Serampore, 115
Slavery, abolition of, 133
Social problems, 37, 38
Spirit, Holy, 18, 22, 49, 70, 73*n.*, 95, 97, 99, 102, 105, 142, 143, 144, 145
Statistics, 92, 154
Superintendents, General, 92
Sustentation Fund, 92, 107*n.*

Taylor, Jeremy, 67
Test Act, 131, 132
Toleration Act, 132
Tottlebank Church, 47
Training of ministers, 61–63, 104, 105 106

Uniformity, Act of, 129
Unity of Free Churches, 11

Worship, 93–97